The Method of
Melville's Short Fiction

*For Karen, and our loving parents,
and for my teacher, Arlin Turner*

The Method of
Melville's Short
Fiction

R. Bruce Bickley, Jr.

1975
Duke University Press
Durham, N.C.

© 1969, 1975, Duke University Press

L.C.C. card no. 74–28904

I.S.B.N. 0–8223–0334–5

Printed in the United States
of America by Heritage Printers, Inc.

Contents

Acknowledgments

In the past few years I have explored ideas in this study with several colleagues and students. However, I would especially like to thank Jerry Gerber and Buford Jones of Duke University, who taught me more about literary method than they may have realized, and my students in American Romanticism at Florida State, who challenged me to see as much about literature as they had seen. Finally, as the dedication suggests, it is Arlin Turner's example as a teacher and scholar and his good counsel over the years that have brought this book to fruition.

I should also like to express my gratitude to Ashbel Brice of Duke University Press for his support of this project and to Bill Hicks and Joanne Ferguson for editing and proofreading.

I am grateful to Kenneth Walter Cameron for permission to use portions of my essay, "The Minor Fiction of Hawthorne and Melville," *American Transcendental Quarterly*, 14 (Spring 1972), 149–52, in chapters two, three, and six. I should also like to thank Jack Meathenia for permission to use portions of my article, "The Triple Thrust of Satire in Melville's Short Stories: Society, the Narrator, and the Reader," *Studies in American Humor*, 1 (Jan. 1975), 172–79, in chapters four and five.

Preface

Since the publication of Richard Harter Fogle's *Melville's Shorter Tales* in 1960,[1] scholarship on Melville's short fiction has proliferated almost too rapidly for acknowledgment and review, much less for proper evaluation. The critical attention paid to "Bartleby" illustrates the point. Note one scholar's half-serious recounting of sources and parallels used to interpret the tale:

> In an attempt to illuminate some aspect of the story or other, critics have cited parallels or sources or influences in the Bible, Hawthorne, Poe, Emerson, Thoreau, Dostoevski, Gogol, Chekhov, Camus, Kafka, Kierkegaard, Buber, Pascal, Montaigne, and Shakespeare. The lawyer-narrator has been related in some fashion to Melville's brother Allen, his uncle Peter Gansevoort, his father-in-law Chief Justice Lemuel Shaw of Massachusetts, Evert Duyckinck, Everyman, the Prophet Jonah, Captain "Starry" Vere, Captain Amasa Delano, and the Lord God Jehovah. Bartleby himself has been related to Christ, to one of the least of Christ's brethren, to Everyman, Benito Cereno, Billy Budd, the Confidence Man, Ishmael, Ahab, Pierre, Plotinus Plinlimmon, Israel Potter, Pip, Hunilla, a tragic white-faced clown, a Buddhist monk, a sannyasi Hindu monk, Natty Bumppo, Mahatma Ghandi, Job, Teufelsdröckh, Holmes's Elsie Venner, Thoreau, Poe's William Wilson, Walter Mitty, and Melville himself.[2]

1. Norman, Okla.: Univ. of Oklahoma Press, 1960.
2. Gordon E. Bigelow, "The Problem of Symbolist Form in Mel-

Despite its volume and resourcefulness, however, I am convinced that the short story scholarship remains inadequate; hence this book. We have yet to look carefully enough at the method of Melville's short fiction as a collection—specifically, at the techniques that Melville experimented with during the four-year period of literary reorientation that followed the popular failures of *Moby-Dick* and *Pierre*, and at the ways in which these techniques shaped his complex vision artistically.[3] This study relocates Melville in the context of his

ville's 'Bartleby the Scrivener,' " *Modern Language Quarterly*, 31 (Sept. 1970), 345–46.

3. The most helpful study of the tales prior to Fogle's book is Charles G. Hoffmann's brief survey of the structure and dramatic form of the magazine stories, "The Shorter Fiction of Herman Melville," *South Atlantic Quarterly*, 52 (July 1953), 414–30. Two book-length studies of the tales have been published since Fogle, along with several articles; with two exceptions, these works are only of limited usefulness in analyzing Melville's technique. Kingsley Widmer considers patterns of nihilistic despair in "Bartleby," "Benito Cereno," and *Billy Budd* in *The Ways of Nihilism: A Study of Herman Melville's Short Novels* (Los Angeles: Ritchie and Simon, 1970). The other full-length study, of style and structure, remains untranslated: Klaus Ensslen, *Melvilles Erzählungen* (Heidelberg: C. Winter, 1966).

Of the articles published since 1960 on the short stories as a group, three focus on philosophical or thematic issues: Judith Slater, "The Domestic Adventurer in Melville's Tales," *American Literature*, 37 (Nov. 1965), 267–79; Marie A. Campbell, "A Quiet Crusade: Melville's Tales of the Fifties," *American Transcendental Quarterly*, 7 (Summer 1970), 8–12; and Scott Donaldson, "The Dark Truth of *The Piazza Tales*," *PMLA*, 85 (Oct. 1970), 1082–86. Slater's article is suggestive, and I will have occasion to refer to it later. Bert C. Bach's "Melville's Theatrical Mask: The Role of Narrative Perspective in his Short Fiction," *Studies in the Literary Imagination*, 2 (April 1969), 43–55, has also helped me focus my discussion.

Good analytical commentary on Melville's method in the tales is found in the introductions and notes to three editions of the stories: Jay Leyda's *Complete Stories of Herman Melville* (New York: Random House, 1949); Warner Berthoff's *Great Short Works of Herman Melville* (New York: Harper and Row [1970]); Hershel Parker's *Shorter Works of Hawthorne and Melville* (Columbus, Ohio: Charles E. Merrill, 1972).

Of the nine unpublished dissertations completed prior to 1972 that give primary emphasis to Melville's magazine fiction, six focus on mat-

short story writing, with reference both to his own fictional methods within the genre and to the literary influences that would affect his technique. Even as Melville was experimenting with structure, narration, and characterization in accordance with his own literary predispositions, he continued to turn, as was his wont, to appropriate source materials. Sources for "The Encantadas" and "Benito Cereno" have been documented, and the search for Bartleby's origins continues apace, but insufficient attention has been paid to Melville's use of the short stories and sketches of his contemporaries. In particular, this study will examine how Melville drew upon Irving's and Hawthorne's works as he gave artistic form to his short fiction.

While analyzing what Wayne Booth calls the "rhetorical resources" which the author uses as he "tries, consciously or unconsciously, to impose his fictional world upon the reader,"[4] this examination of Melville's stories is intended to be more than an analysis of technique alone. Ultimately, it seeks to penetrate into the complex interior of Melville's fictive vision and to put into clearer focus the essential meanings of his tales, for with Melville it is dramatically true that technique is vision. The pattern of confrontation in "Bartleby," for instance, or

---

ters of technique or literary influence: John Paul Runden, "Imagery in Melville's Shorter Fiction: 1853–1856," Indiana, 1952; Norman Eugene Hoyle, "Melville as a Magazinist," Duke, 1960; James Devers, "Melancholy, Myth, and Symbol in Melville's 'Benito Cereno': An Interpretive Study," UCLA, 1968; Robert Alan McQuitty, "A Rhetorical Approach to Melville's 'Bartleby,' 'Benito Cereno,' and *Billy Budd*," Syracuse, 1968; my own dissertation, "Literary Influences and Technique in Melville's Short Fiction: 1853–1856," Duke, 1969; Wallace McVay Christy, "The Shock of Recognition: A Psycho-Literary Study of Hawthorne's Influence on Melville's Short Fiction," Brown, 1970.

Two commentaries on Melvillean irony and narrative form that have especially stimulated my thinking are Paul Brodtkorb, Jr.'s *Ishmael's White World: A Phenomenological Reading of Moby-Dick* (New Haven and London: Yale Univ. Press, 1965), and John Seelye's *Melville: The Ironic Diagram* (Evanston, Ill.: Northwestern Univ. Press, 1970).

4. Preface, *The Rhetoric of Fiction* (Chicago: Univ. of Chicago Press, 1961).

the ironic quest of "The Piazza" determines and controls meaning. To take another example, Melville's careful manipulation of narrative tone in even a minor work like "Jimmy Rose" reveals the sophistication of his art during his magazine career. My study is only incidentally biographical, as Leon Howard and Warner Berthoff have thoroughly recreated the historical and psychological setting of Melville's short fiction writing.[5] Yet this book does make the case for the continuing intellectual and artistic growth of Melville the man, despite the disillusionment that attended his loss of audience after *Moby-Dick* and *Pierre*. Like Berthoff, I am convinced that Melville's publications between 1853 and 1856 in fact show more discipline, if not a higher level of craftsmanship, than did the earlier novels.[6] Thus, in studying the method of Melville's art, this book implicitly stresses Melville's creative power and originality of conception and execution.

To some extent, my study combines a topical and a chronological approach to the sixteen stories and sketches Melville composed from 1853 to 1856.[7] Since Melville was essentially an experimenter with the form and method of the short story during his magazine career, my approach to his stories is based primarily upon analysis of his literary craftsmanship in artistically related tales. Chapters one and two preserve the chronology of Melville's initial ventures into the genre from "Fragments from a Writing-Desk, No. 2" in 1839 to "Agatha" and "Bartleby" in 1852–53. In chapters three through eight chronology yields to methodology, as I examine Melville's use of several types of first-person irony, his third-person narra-

5. Howard, *Herman Melville* (Berkeley and Los Angeles: Univ. of California Press, 1967); Berthoff, *The Example of Melville* (Princeton: Princeton Univ. Press, 1962).

6. *The Example of Melville*, pp. 57, 59.

7. I will include in my study "The 'Gees," published in *Harper's* for March 1856, and collected in the Constable Edition, Vol. XIII; Jay Leyda chose not to reprint this sketch in *The Complete Stories of Herman Melville*. "The Two Temples" remained unpublished in Melville's lifetime, although he had submitted it to *Putnam's* (see chapter five).

tives, and his experiments with form in "The Encantadas" and the quest stories. The Epilogue, finally, provides a general estimate of the importance of Melville's short stories in his pursuit of the craft of fiction, from *Typee* to *Billy Budd*.

R. B. B., Jr.

Bibliographical Notes

All references to Melville's magazine tales and sketches of the 1850's, with the exception of "The 'Gees," will be to the Modern Library edition, *Selected Writings of Herman Melville* (New York: Random House, 1952). The short works in this text were printed from the plates used in preparing Jay Leyda's carefully edited *The Complete Stories of Herman Melville* (New York: Random House, 1949). Quotations from the Modern Library text will be abbreviated *SW*, followed by the page number. References to "The 'Gees" will be to *Billy Budd and Other Prose Pieces*, vol. XIII in *The Works of Herman Melville* (London: Constable and Co., 1922–24). References to *Typee, Omoo, Mardi, Redburn, White-Jacket,* and *Pierre* will be to the definitive Northwestern University Press and Newberry Library edition (Evanston and Chicago: 1968–71). References to *Moby-Dick* and *The Confidence-Man* will be to the Norton Critical Editions (New York: W. W. Norton and Co., 1967, 1971, respectively). References to Melville's letters will be to Merrell R. Davis and William H. Gilman, eds., *The Letters of Herman Melville* (New Haven: Yale University Press, 1960). References to other writings by Melville will be cited routinely in the text.

The Method of
Melville's Short Fiction

I

Experiments in Narrative: Structure and Vision

Narrative Technique through White-Jacket

In Chapter 180 of *Mardi*, Babbalanja the philosopher discusses Lombardo's method for composing his "crazy" work, the Koztanza: "When Lombardo set about his work, he knew not what it would become. He did not build himself in with plans; he wrote right on; and so doing, got deeper and deeper into himself; and like a resolute traveler, plunging through baffling woods, at last was rewarded for his toils. 'In good time,' saith he, in his autobiography, 'I came out into a serene, sunny, ravishing region; full of sweet scents, singing birds, wild plaints, roguish laughs, prophetic voices. Here we are at last, then,' he cried; 'I have created the creative'" (*Mardi*, p. 595). This passage is intriguing for two reasons. It characterizes Melville's most ambitious novels, for "wild plaints," "roguish laughs," and "prophetic voices" make *Mardi*, *Moby-Dick*, *Pierre*, and *The Confidence-Man* the books they are. What is more significant, the quotation serves as an apologia for Melville's Romantic art. Melville's improvisational method led him progressively "deeper into himself" and into his sources of creative power; this was the only way he could write.

When King Abrazza protests that the Koztanza "lacks cohesion" and that it is "wild, unconnected, all episode," Babbalanja replies in a now celebrated passage: "And so is Mardi itself:—nothing but episodes; valleys and hills; rivers, digressing from plains; vines, roving all over; boulders and diamonds;

3

flowers and thistles; forests and thickets; and, here and there, fens and moors. And so, the world in the Koztanza" (*Mardi*, p. 597). The image of the novel as microcosm suggests *Mardi* itself, as well as *White-Jacket*, *Moby-Dick*, and *The Confidence-Man*. But Babbalanja's comment on the digressive and episodic structure of the Koztanza also has important implications for the short fiction. Critics have often observed Melville's proclivity to build his novels around smaller units of composition. Episodic structure is as old as Homer, and it is basic to the storyteller's sense of his art. For Melville, Warner Berthoff theorizes, storytelling is a kind of "social rite," in which the teller seeks to engage the reader in a "confederating" and "civil process." Uppermost in the teller's mind is the desire to entertain and to make the reader an aficionado of tales: hence the search for variety and flexibility in tale-telling.[1] With Melville, also, there seems to be a certain impatience with the form of the novel; thus he attempts to move the reader, with a minimum of fatigue, along a varied terrain of narrative and exposition.

Although literary reorientation and a considerable refocusing of energies would still be required, Melville's own best instincts, as well as his previous literary practice, had in a sense already begun to prepare him for short story writing. Specifically, Melville's experiments with structure, narrative, and imagery in earlier works anticipate in important ways the method of his magazine tales.

Technically, Melville began his literary career in 1839, as an essayist and short fiction writer. "Fragments from a Writing-Desk," No. 1 and No. 2, were published in the *Democratic Press and Lansingburgh Advertiser* for May 4 and 18; they consisted of a Chesterfieldian letter on style, social artifice, and beauty, and an Oriental tale that seems to have been written as a parody of Byron, Thomas Moore, and the *Arabian Nights*. The second "Fragment" is the more ambitious work, and it reveals a great deal about Melville's instincts as a fiction writer.

1. *Great Short Works of Herman Melville*, pp. 10, 12.

While it fulfills the structural requirements of the short story (a limited set of characters, and a self-contained plot with a complication and a resolution), the "Fragment" also shows Melville's attraction to the quest as a basic literary form. Furthermore, the tale illustrates Melville's penchant for ironic narration and his early skill in using imagery to reflect character and reinforce theme.

In this piece of juvenilia, a mysterious woman hands the narrator a message that commands him to follow her. After a lengthy journey in which he is prevented from approaching his guide to ask her any questions, the narrator finds himself in an opulently furnished boudoir; a fulsome Eastern beauty beckons to him from a couch, he is captivated, his loyalty to "another" forgotten, he kisses her passionately, and then he discovers that his sultry enchantress is "DUMB AND DEAF!"[2] Melville had already discovered the viability of the quest as a literary motif, both for creating suspense and for providing structure. Furthermore, the ironic reversal of a quester's experience would later prove to be paradigmatic. Melville's greatest works are studies in thwarted quests and unfulfilled, or self-destroying, questers. As John Seelye has diagrammed the characteristic Melvillean pattern, the quester's "forward thrust of inquiry" and the generally linear design of the narrative again and again ironically resolve themselves into the circle of incompleteness, failure, or relativism and ambiguity.[3] Of course, the ironic quest for a mysterious woman is the central theme in *Mardi, Pierre*, and "The Piazza" as well.

Melville uses first-person narration to intensify the irony of the quest. The tale has immediacy and a certain spontaneous realism, despite its archly allusive texture and stilted language; most important, Melville's narrator is an ironic persona, the

2. Quotations from "Fragment No. 2" are from William H. Gilman, *Melville's Early Life and Redburn* (New York: New York Univ. Press, 1951), Appendix B, pp. 265–71. Gilman, pp. 109–20, thoroughly discusses the style and texture of the two "Fragments," and my analysis of "Fragment No. 2" is partially indebted to his.

3. *Melville: The Ironic Diagram*, pp. 5, 7, and passim.

dupe of his own impulsive nature and romantic fascination with the mysterious and unusual, to say nothing of the sensuous. The story begins *in medias res*, and its opening is our earliest example of Melville's instinctive skill in the "comedy of involuntary gesture," to borrow a term that Berthoff uses to characterize the tales of the 'fifties:[4]

> "Confusion seize the Greek!" exclaimed I, as wrathfully rising from my chair, I flung my ancient Lexicon across the room, and seizing my hat and cane, and throwing on my cloak, I sallied out into the clear air of heaven. The bracing coolness of an April evening calmed my aching temples. . . . ("Fragment," p. 265)

Melville sustains the spontaneity and humor of his narrative by two methods, which would later characterize his most accomplished storytelling: by psychological portraiture, in which the first-person narrator displays his own eccentricities and "hypoes," and involuntarily satirizes himself, and by the drama of physical activity. Having calmed his emotions, the narrator was resting by the riverside when the mysterious figure dropped something at his feet. Note how Melville, through both physical and psychological description, dramatizes his narrator's impulsive nature: " 'Certes!' cried I, springing up, 'here is a spice of the marvelous!' and stooping down, I picked up an elegant little, rose-coloured, lavender-scented billet-doux . . ." ("Fragment," p. 265). The letter is signed "Inamorata," and it enjoins the narrator to follow the strange guide. "The deuce I will!" is his instinctive response, for as a man of the world he sees himself as always superior to women; but then he suddenly changes his mind and pursues her through the darkening city. By the end of his journey the narrator has cut quite a comic figure: gasping for breath and generally fatigued, he "desperately" flings off his mantle.

4. Prefatory note to "The Lightning-Rod Man," in *Great Short Works of Herman Melville*, p. 187.

Still unable to catch the fleet-footed girl, he curses and stamps the ground in rage: "What! to be thwarted by a woman? Peradventure, baffled by a girl? Confusion! It was too bad! To be outgeneraled, routed, defeated, by a mere rib of the earth? It was not to be borne!" ("Fragment," p. 267). Overcome by his "hypoes," like Ishmael he even contemplates suicide, but he manages to continue his quest.

The last half of the story augments ironic portraiture with imagery. Young Melville flexes his literary muscles perhaps better than he realizes in leading his narrator through a sexually symbolic archway of "swelling" foliage, and "through a long corridor" to a low door, behind which he finds the voluptuously furnished apartment and the equally voluptuous maiden. His senses are "overwhelmed" and he is hers, but only until he discovers her secret. The quest is complete, yet the narrator is its ironic and comically grotesque victim.

A variety of anecdotes, digressive stories, and "histories" in *Typee* through *Pierre* could qualify as rudimentary short fiction, although none of the examples one might cite, except for "The Town-Ho's Story," is framed or developed with the care that Melville used in "Fragment No. 2." The reason, of course, is that Melville's yarn-spinning in these books is part of a larger pattern of anthropological sketching, social commentary, allegory, autobiographical narrative, and, in *Moby-Dick* and *Pierre*, metaphysical speculation. Thus the anecdote of the Queen of Nukuheva in *Typee*, the story of Toby as sequel to the second edition of that novel, the account of Dr. Long Ghost's "caper" with the sailor and his sea chest in *Omoo*, "A Hunting Ramble with Zeke" in the same book, or the story of the "massacre" of the beards in *White-Jacket* are entertaining, but hardly compelling as storytelling. More successful as quasi-short fiction are the history of Samoa, Annatoo, and the brigantine *Parki*, in *Mardi*, the Harry Bolton interlude in *Redburn*, the gams of the *Jeroboam*, the *Samuel Enderby*, and the *Rachel* in *Moby-Dick*, and the story of Isabel, in *Pierre*. In these short narratives Melville builds tension and character conflict around details of setting, and each tale could conceivably stand alone as a self-contained story.

After the "Fragment," "The Town-Ho's Story" and the Agatha letters were Melville's best warm-up exercises for the magazine fiction, as I shall indicate below. Nevertheless, the episodic novels through *Moby-Dick* afforded him considerable practice in the technique he would consistently draw upon from 1853 to 1856: ironic first-person narration. In all of his works from "Fragment No. 2" to *Moby-Dick*, and in fourteen out of sixteen magazine stories and sketches, Melville used as protagonists first-person narrators who were, to a greater or lesser extent, ironically portrayed. In a sense, too, *Pierre* and "Benito Cereno" are "honorary" first-person narratives, since Melville for the most part limits authorial privilege to the consciousness of Pierre and Delano alone; this would leave only "The Bell-Tower" as legitimate third-person narrative. The art of ironic portraiture, my study will argue, reaches its peak in short stories like "Bartleby," "Cock-A-Doodle-Doo!" and "The Piazza," and in a very real way Melville's entire career is a preparation for his masterful use of the ironic confessional mode in the magazine works. The comedy of involuntary gesture that begins in the "Fragment" appears repeatedly in *Typee* through *Moby-Dick*. Although Melville's narrators may partially realize their own limitations, inadequacies, or foolishness, the point is that the last laugh, and the larger perception, are generally left to the reader.

In *Typee* Tommo's vanity at being the center of attention in the valley is seen for what it is, when the taboo savage Marnoo arrives in the village and all the natives desert the narrator for him. "I felt not a little piqued. The glory of Tommo is departed, thought I, and the sooner he removes from the valley the better. These were my feelings at the moment, and they were prompted by that glorious principle inherent in all heroic natures—the strong-rooted determination to have the biggest share of the pudding or go without any of it" (*Typee*, p. 137). The ironic distance between reader and narrator often fluctuates in Melville, and we are perhaps less apt to laugh at the paranoia Tommo develops over the possibility of being tattooed by the village artist, Karky. "Horrified at the bare thought of being rendered hideous for life," Tommo tries tactfully to decline Karky's solicitations, but when the artist uses his forefinger to lay out some possible patterns on his face, Tommo's instincts for self-preservation overcome all other considerations. As he had done in the "Fragment" and as he would do frequently in the short fiction, Melville builds comedy around physical action: "half wild with terror and indignation, I succeeded in breaking away . . . and fled . . ." (*Typee*, pp. 218, 219). Trying to maintain the balance between humor and horror, Melville keeps putting Karky in Tommo's path: "Several times I met him in various parts of the valley, and, invariably, whenever he descried me, he came running after me with his mallet and chisel, flourishing them about my face as if he longed to begin. What an object he would have made of me!" (*Typee*, p. 219).

Omoo is less unified than Melville's first novel, and the narrator's character is only barely developed. Yet Melville continues, in his best improvisatory comic and dramatic mode, to give his writing a double-vision of sorts, playing the reader's perspective against the narrator's. Thus when a saucy but beautiful native girl dashes into the Calabooza, where Omoo and his companions are being temporarily detained, and laughs at several of the men, the narrator throws his bedraggled figure into the most graceful attitude he can assume. Leaning his head upon his hand, he summons up an abstracted, sentimental expression, and, feeling his face flush, realizes that the girl is looking at him—and, so far, happily, not a sound of derision:

> Delicious thought! she was moved at the sight of me.
> I could stand it no longer, but started up. Lo! there she
> was; her great hazel eyes rounding and rounding in her

head, like two stars, her whole frame in a merry quiver, and an expression about the mouth that was sudden and violent death to any thing like sentiment.

The next moment she spun around, and, bursting from peal to peal of laughter, went racing out of the Calabooza; and, in mercy to me, never returned. (*Omoo*, p. 130)

The pattern of ironic laughter is repeated elsewhere in the novel. Omoo, dressed in a voluminous tunic and a turban, once seeks to impress two English ladies with his good breeding. He advances "winningly" and bids them good evening, when "Hysterics and hartshorn! who would have thought it? The young lady screamed, and the old one came near fainting." Melville concludes the comic episode with characteristic attention to his narrator's physical reflex action when under stress: "As for myself," says Omoo, "I retreated, in double quick time; and scarcely drew breath, until safely housed in the Calabooza" (*Omoo*, p. 167).

In the early portions of *Mardi*, Melville gave further development to the narrative protagonist as ironic persona. Here Melville even allows his narrator to sin, in the name of pride and covetousness. Taji, having impulsively murdered the priest Aleema to rescue Yillah, lets her believe that he is a godlike creature; furthermore, he feeds her false stories about the youthful experiences they supposedly shared, in order to make her his. Taji knows in his heart that he has only rationalized the murder of Aleema, and he continues to feel guilt over what he has done and is haunted by the priest's image. One could argue, finally, that Taji deserves the ironic quest that the fates have set for him; he has no moral right to possess Yillah and hence must forever pursue her phantom "over an endless sea." The fate of the lawyer in "Bartleby" is less severe, of course, but the same kind of ironic distancing between Melville's narrator and the truth is present. Can the lawyer's consciousness and conscience ever be freed, completely, of the forlorn image of Bartleby, the man he may have allowed to die?

10

As Melville expanded his vision in his allegorical romance, his conception of his narrator's role enlarged accordingly. As would be the case with Ishmael in *Moby-Dick*, Taji becomes more stage manager than dramatized persona once Melville has his novel well under way. A complete description of Melville's narrative improvisations in *Mardi* is almost impossible. Not only does Taji himself repeatedly subordinate his quest for Yillah to poetic, philosophic, and allegorical musings, but he also frequently hands over the narrative to Mohi, Babbalanja, Yoomy, and King Media, who, in turn, hold forth in their own styles, and on their own particular subjects—history, or philosophy, or poetic art, or politics. In many ways, then, this experimental romance looks forward to the multiple visions of Melville's gallery of short fiction narrators of the 'fifties— each with his own personality, value system, and favorite subject, whether it be lonely scriveners, or Christian charity, or corpulent chimneys. In addition, one could probably draw direct lines of influence between the Mardian archipelago and that of the Encantadas, where narrator-guides take the reader on symbolical island tours across landscapes of humanity and inhumanity, freedom and slavery, and enchantment and reality.

Redburn and *White-Jacket* were written back-to-back in the spring and summer of 1849, and they are generally considered as parallel works of art, with parallel subjects. *Redburn*, however, is more explicitly a *Bildungsroman*, stressing the youth and innocence of its narrator and the shock of experience, while *White-Jacket* is chiefly a documentary narrative and survey of naval life, invested with important symbolical overtones. The two novels, despite Melville's apologies for them as mere hackwork, show a further development of rhetorical double vision. Like Dickens in *David Copperfield*, Melville in *Redburn* retrospectively reconstructs Wellingborough's adventures using the persona of the now mature man to point up, ironically and comically, Wellingborough's youthful mistakes, hypoes, and misconceptions. *White-Jacket* is a more "immediate" book in the sense that the narrator seems primarily to be writing things down as they happen, although there is some foreshadowing about the end of the troublesome jacket. Thus the ironic play between narrator and reader in *White-Jacket* is somewhat more subtle than that in *Redburn*. As he would do in *Moby-Dick* and in most of the short stories, Melville in *White-Jacket* obliges the reader to discover the limits or biases of the narrator's perceptions. White-Jacket is a loner, a self-styled Ishmael who ironically reinforces his own isolation, in the name of identity and individuality, by insisting on wearing his white windbreaker despite all logical and humane arguments to the contrary. Symbolically, his jacket almost kills him, and his rebirth after his fall into the "speechless profound" of the sea (*White-Jacket*, p. 392) marks his emergence as a mature man, redeemed from his own egocentricity. A major issue in the later short stories will be the extent to which Melville's narrators discover their own egocentricity for what it is.

"The Town-Ho's Story" and "Agatha"

White-Jacket, while in some ways a more tedious and less entertaining novel than *Redburn*, marks a turning point in Melville's rhetoric of fiction. From the more obvious kinds of humor and irony displayed in the earlier works and in *Redburn*, Melville shifts his angle of vision in his fifth novel. Taken together, the allegory of *Mardi* and the symbolism of *White-Jacket* set the stage for the Ishmaelian vision, both in its expansiveness and complex ironies and in its qualifications of what man is privileged to know.[5] And Ishmael, in turn, prepares the way for the multiple visions of the short fiction narrators.

In characteristic fashion, Melville introduces Ishmael as narrator ironically: he is another rover with yet another set of hypoes and humorous idiosyncrasies. He is out of money and is self-conscious about his patched appearance. Furthermore,

5. See Brodtkorb, *Ishmael's White World*, passim.

he needs the sea to vent off a latent belligerence as well as suicidal tendencies; but, a philosopher at heart, he also admits that he enjoys getting "social" with the things that most horrify. Ishmael's greatest hypo is the whiteness of the whale, and thus Melville's ironic portrait of his narrator works rhetorically to expand the meaning of his novel: the whale's whiteness is Ishmael's own tormenting and "ungraspable phantom of life," and, finally, he makes it ours, too.

Ishmael as dramatized first-person narrator soon becomes absorbed into the larger omniscient vision of the novel, but the inconsistency is not troublesome. We are so quickly taken with his personality, quirks and all, that when Ishmael turns stage manager we instinctively yield him the authority to do so. For Melville's comedy of involuntary gesture has made Ishmael human, and therefore real; the reader enjoys watching him and, of more importance, listening to his ideas.

He is finicky about having to sleep with a strange harpooner at the Spouter Inn, and it takes him a good half-hour of futile rearranging of benches and chairs downstairs to convince him that he'd be better off to chance it upstairs with Queequeg, after all. He is the dupe of Peter Coffin's humorous gamesmanship about Queequeg's character, and, later, Peleg enjoys keeping him off guard about the identity of the captain of the *Pequod* and the advisability of going to sea at all. With his eye always open to the comic possibilities of human reflexes, Melville provides a delightful portrait of Ishmael's attempts, in advance, to fathom Queequeg's character by looking through the harpooner's personal belongings. He finds what looks like a large door mat with a hole in the middle in Queequeg's chest. "But could it be possible," Ishmael wonders, "that any sober harpooner would get into a door mat, and parade the streets of any Christian town in that sort of guise?" He tries the shaggy mat on and ventures a glance in the mirror: "I never saw such a sight in my life. I tore myself out of it in such a hurry that I gave myself a kink in the neck" (*Moby-Dick*, p. 28).

Touches like these make Ishmael personal and alive. He is one of us, but at the same time his voice of experience carries us where we have never been. Therefore we listen to Ishmael when, "for [his] humor's sake," in Chapter 54 he retells the story of the *Town-Ho*, in the style in which he once narrated it to a circle of friends at Lima. The story itself reports the second of the nine gams in *Moby-Dick*. As critics have indicated, all of the gams bear in some way on the themes or plot of the novel,[6] and "The Town-Ho's Story," although Melville left its ultimate meaning ambiguous, foreshadows the final confrontation of Ahab and the white whale. Critics have also recognized, as did Harper and Brothers, who published the episode separately to puff their forthcoming edition of *Moby-Dick*,[7] that the gam can stand as a story complete in its own right. The *Town-Ho* episode was a "secret" narrative, and its final outcome was kept from Ahab's ears. This accounts in part for its dramatic intensity; in fact, the story is one of Melville's most sustained pieces of dramatic writing, along with the three-day chase in *Moby-Dick* and portions of *Billy Budd*.[8]

6. See James Dean Young, "The Nine Gams of the *Pequod*," *American Literature*, 25 (Jan. 1954), 449–63; William K. Spofford, "Melville's Ambiguities: A Re-evaluation of 'The Town-Ho's Story,'" *American Literature*, 41 (May 1969), 264–70.

7. *Harper's New Monthly Magazine*, 3 (Oct. 1851), 658–65. The story was also published separately in the Baltimore *Weekly Sun* for November 8, 1851, and in the Cincinnati *Daily Gazette* in two installments: November 29 and December 6, 1851.

8. Charles R. Anderson, in *Melville in the South Seas* (New York: Columbia Univ. Press, 1939), p. 39, says that Melville could have found the germ for the *Town-Ho*'s story in a yarn in J. Ross Browne's *Etchings of a Whaling Cruise*, which Melville had reviewed for *The Literary World* in 1847. Ishmael and his shipmates had heard the *Town-Ho*'s story during a gam, just as Browne had listened to "Bob Grimsley's Ghost" during a gam. Both stories concern a mate who had conceived a mortal hatred for a common sailor, and both involve a type of just recompense, or judgment, which falls on the mate because of his malevolence. Melville combined the *Etchings* story and fragments from various yarns he had heard to create the final tale.

Ishmael permits himself two digressions, about the Great Lakes and the Erie Canal, but otherwise he holds rigidly to the story, which he relates in the third person. To borrow Wayne Booth's terminology, Melville emphasizes "showing": Ishmael had not been a participator in the events, and he chose to relate them objectively and dramatically. Despite more than a score of parenthetic "gentlemen," asides which remind us that the oral tradition of storytelling is at work, the story maintains its momentum to the end. Like Conrad's Marlow, half a century later, Melville's Ishmael tells his story to a small coterie of interested friends, taking a page or two to set the stage for the storytelling. Melville seems to be working almost instinctively with a "frame" for his story, as he would in several of his magazine tales.

Limits of time and space make it impractical for the short story writer to attempt a complete analysis of character, so Melville, much like Poe and Hawthorne, usually focused on selected character traits which would "set up" a story for the reader: a character's motivations precipitate some kind of action, resulting in a climax and conclusion. And there is always the possibility that chance, or Fate, may intervene to shape events. This is not to say that Melville could not work "backwards," as he may very well have done with the *Town-Ho* story: hearing a yarn and developing characters' personalities to suit the sequence of events. He used this technique in the Agatha story, in fact.

Thus Ishmael introduces his story in terms of the motivations and personality traits of its chief characters. The tale will have to do with "the brutal overbearing of Radney, the mate" and "the bitterly provoked vengeance" of his subordinate Steelkilt. Ishmael speaks in general, and then specific, terms about what will provoke Radney's resentment of Steelkilt:

"Now, as you well know, it is not seldom the case in this conventional world of ours—watery or otherwise; that when a person placed in command over his fellow-men finds one of them to be very significantly his superior in general pride of manhood, straightway against that man he conceives an unconquerable dislike and bitterness; and if he have a chance he will pull down and pulverize that subaltern's tower, and make a little heap of dust of it. Be this conceit of mine as it may, gentlemen, at all events Steelkilt was a tall and noble animal with a head like a Roman, and a flowing golden beard like the tasseled housings of your last viceroy's snorting charger; and a brain, and a heart, and a soul in him, gentlemen, which had made Steelkilt Charlemagne, had he been born son to Charlemagne's father. But Radney, the mate, was ugly as a mule; yet as hardy, as stubborn, as malicious. He did not love Steelkilt, and Steelkilt knew it." (*Moby-Dick*, p. 211)

The rest of the story dramatizes, through dialogue and character confrontation, Radney's humiliation of Steelkilt, Steelkilt's calculated revenge, and then Radney's destruction by Moby-Dick before Steelkilt could execute his plans. It was as if Radney had been brought to justice (and, in turn, Steelkilt spared a murder charge) by an "inverted visitation of one of those so called judgments of God," as Ishmael ambiguously observes (*Moby-Dick*, p. 208).

In "The Town-Ho's Story" Melville had practice, two years prior to his magazine phase, in meeting many of the structural demands of the short story. The circumstances of the *Town-Ho* episode seemed to call for a dramatic, self-contained short narrative; thanks partially to his own literary instincts and partially to his reading and yarn-collecting, Melville found that he could successfully develop both plot and character within the more limited framework of the tale.

Even more significant for the student of Melville's short fiction technique are the celebrated "Agatha letters" written by Melville to Hawthorne during the autumn of 1852—about nine months before he began to compose "Bartleby." While

"The Town-Ho's Story" illustrates Melville's use of short story structure, the Agatha material reveals his innate skill in fusing character, image, and theme. Melville wrote Hawthorne on 13 August that during a visit to Nantucket in July he had met John H. Clifford, Attorney General for Massachusetts, and that the two of them had talked, so he recalled, of "the great patience, & endurance, & resignedness of the women of the island in submitting so uncomplainingly to the long, long absences of their sailor husbands" (*Letters*, pp. 153–54). Their conversation reminded Clifford of a case concerning a young woman who had been deserted by her seafaring husband. Clifford responded to Melville's sudden interest in his story by mailing to him, soon afterwards, his personal detailed memorandum of the case, and Melville had turned the narrative over in his mind, thinking that "a regular story" could be "founded on these striking incidents." Yet the project seemed more suited to Hawthorne's abilities (Melville mentioned, in fact, that one of the characters in the Agatha account reminded him of Wakefield):

> with your great power in these things, you can construct a story of remarkable interest out of this material. . . . You have a skeleton of actual reality to build about with fulness & veins & beauty. And if I thought I could do it as well as you, why, I should not let you have it. (*Letters*, p. 157)

In his initial Agatha letter to Hawthorne, Melville not only enclosed Clifford's memorandum but also some 1500 words of observations and suggestions about bringing the story out of the lawyer's prosaic, documentary account into its potential "rounded & beautified & thoroughly developed state" (*Letters*, p. 155). On 25 October 1852 he jotted down for Hawthorne's use some further reflections on the story. In early November the two met in Concord and discussed Agatha again, and in the final Agatha letter, sometime after 25 November 1852, we learn that Hawthorne had recommended that Melville write

the story himself. Not surprisingly, Melville stated that he was beginning "immediately." Although no completed "Story of Agatha" has turned up, Melville used some of the Agatha material in the tale of Hunilla in "The Encantadas" a year and a half later (see chapter seven, below); also, as has been frequently pointed out, the "Agatha theme" of patience and endurance was a dominant one in the magazine tales. It is obvious that Melville continued for some years to be affected by her tale and its possibilities for art.

The Agatha material is uniquely valuable because at no other place in Melville's short fiction do we find a source for a story still in the process of being shaped and rendered as art. The letters show that Melville pays great attention to characterization; also, one discovers how he intuitively molds descriptive backdrop into image and symbol, to support the developing themes of the tale. What was originally a bare, factual "skeleton of actual reality" is being shaped, before the reader's eyes, into a profound study of a "trial of humanity."

Melville saw that the incidents in Agatha's life were dramatic enough as they stood, so he left the chain of events in the documents essentially unchanged. Clifford's and Melville's accounts tell of the storm off the coast of Pembroke, Massachusetts, of how young Agatha Hatch cares for the shipwrecked sailor Robertson (Melville accidentally calls him "Robinson"), and of how the two come to be married. For added drama and poignancy Melville suggests that Agatha actually save the sailor and that he be the only survivor; neither of these were factual events. Two years pass, and Robertson, leaving his wife pregnant, starts off to find employment. He is gone for seventeen years, however. During this time he takes another wife, returning to Agatha only when the second wife dies. Agatha refuses his offers of money and a new home, and he goes away, marries a third wife, and eventually dies.

But note how Melville "rounded & beautified" the facts of the story. First of all, and parallel to the technique of "The Town-Ho's Story," he focuses attention on the possible moti-

vations of Robertson's actions. All that Clifford's document had said specifically about Robertson's character was that, in his later years, "he seemed to be a very jealous suspicious man" and that he "must have received a portion of his punishment in this life" (*Letters*, pp. 160, 161). Melville, always a patron of poor ignorant seamen, recommended that

> In estimating the character of Robinson [sic] Charity should be allowed a liberal play. I take exception to that passage from the Diary which says that "*he must have received a portion of his punishment in this life*"—thus hinting of a future supplemental castigation.—I do not at all suppose that his desertion of his wife was a premeditated thing. If it had been so, he would have changed his name, probably, after quitting her.—No: he was a weak man, & his temptations (tho' we know little of them) were strong. The whole sin stole upon him insensibly—so that it would perhaps have been hard for him to settle upon the exact day when he could say to himself, "*Now* I have deserted my wife." (*Letters*, pp. 154–55)

In his second letter Melville refers again to the necessity for "charity" in characterizing Robertson:

> The probable facility with which Robinson first leaves his wife & then takes another, may, possibly, be ascribed to the peculiarly latitudinarian notions, which most sailors have of all tender obligations of that sort. . . . The sense of the obligation of the marriage-vow to Agatha had little weight with him at first. *It* was only when some years of life ashore had passed that his moral sense on that point became developed. (*Letters*, p. 161)

Since the general theme of Melville's hypothetical story appears to be the almost heroic patience and endurance of Agatha, it may seem contradictory that he should place so much emphasis on a "liberal" view of Robertson. However, as Melville wrote Hawthorne in the first letter, there is such "suggestiveness" surrounding Robertson that one should not condemn him immediately, although his desertion was a "sin."

Melville's technique is revealed further in his delineation of Agatha herself. In depicting her, he uses fewer passages of direct description than Clifford had used in his diary; instead, he created her out of the setting, or physical backdrop, of the story. In the Agatha letters, as in "The Encantadas," "Cock-A-Doodle-Doo!" and "Benito Cereno," landscape becomes a telling indicator of character and, in turn, of theme.

Melville suggests that, the day of the shipwreck, the afternoon should be "mild & warm. The sea with an air of solemn deliberation, with an elaborate deliberation, ceremoniously rolls upon the beach" (*Letters*, p. 155). Agatha is reclining on a cliff overlooking the sea, and, like the sea itself, she is "[f]illed with meditations" as she gazes out toward the horizon. A cluster of clouds presages a storm, and "[t]his again gives food for thought" (*Letters*, p. 156). The sea seems to reflect her own pensiveness. Then Melville improvises with symbolic effect:

> Suddenly she catches the long shadow of the cliff cast upon the beach 100 feet beneath her; and now she notes a shadow moving along the shadow. It is cast by a sheep from the pasture. It had advanced to the very edge of the cliff, & is sending a mild innocent glance far out upon the water. Here, in strange & beautiful contrast, we have the innocence of the land placidly eyeing the malignity of the sea. (*Letters*, p. 156)

In case Hawthorne had not made the connection, Melville adds parenthetically: "All this having poetic reference to Agatha & her sea-lover, who is coming in the storm. . . ."

The sheep symbolizes one aspect of Agatha's character, her innocence, and Melville uses another landscape motif—a postbox—to represent her confrontation with time. For seventeen years Agatha pays a daily visit to the rude wooden box, trusting to find a letter from her husband; yet,

As her hopes gradually decay in her, so does the post itself & the little box decay. The post rots in the ground at last. Owing to its being little used—hardly used at all— grass grows rankly about it. . . . At last the post falls. (*Letters*, p. 157)

Here Melville's symbolism seems somewhat contrived, but in the Hunilla story he works more subtly: the rotting mailbox as time symbol is replaced by a piece of sea-worn driftwood, which the deserted Chola widow patiently notched as her calendar.

The Agatha narrative, Melville had written to Hawthorne, was "instinct with significance." The magazine stories, in their finished form, will reveal again and again how Melville turned the latent "significances" of his source materials into art.

Personae and Vision in the Magazine Tales

The mid-nineteenth century reading public generally condemned Melville's best attempts at novel-writing, for it could not stomach the "maniacal" style of *Moby-Dick* or the "blasphemous rhapsody" of *Pierre*. In his magazine stories, however, Melville modified his rhetoric, and, to all appearances, his subject matter; the result was that *The Piazza Tales* drew uniformly favorable reviews and sold respectably.[9] Melville's success with the short story in his own time certainly owed a good deal to his ability to work within the popular magazine

9. The five collected *Putnam's* tales, "Bartleby," "The Lightning-Rod Man," "The Bell-Tower," "The Encantadas," and "Benito Cereno," with "The Piazza" as introductory sketch, sold 1047 copies in the first three months after publication; it took *Harper's* five years to sell 2500 copies of *Moby-Dick*, thirty-five years to sell 1800 copies of *Pierre*. See Merton M. Sealts, Jr., "The Publication of Melville's *Piazza Tales*," *Modern Language Notes*, 59 (Jan. 1944), 56–59; William Charvat, "Melville and the Common Reader," *Studies in Bibliography*, 12 (1959), 41–57; G. Thomas Tanselle, "The Sales of Melville's Books," *Harvard Library Bulletin*, 17 (April 1969), 195–215.

forms of the travel sketch ("The Encantadas"), the gothic story or tale of mystery with a "solution" at the end ("Benito Cereno" and "The Bell-Tower"), the Romantic confessional ("I and My Chimney" and "The Piazza"), and the familiar essay or character sketch ("Bartleby," "Jimmy Rose," or "The Apple-Tree Table"). Yet in the short fiction there was little sacrifice of intellectual integrity, for Melville had discovered ways of concealing larger philosophical (and sometimes ribaldly comical) issues below the more overtly magazinish surface of his stories. At the same time, he found in the compression and discipline that the short story required a new artistic strength.

"Fragments from a Writing-Desk," "The Town-Ho's Story," and "Agatha" contributed to Melville's mastery of character development, structure, and imagery within the self-contained story. Also fundamental to his method in the magazine tales was ironic narration, learned in part from his earlier experiments with first-person narrative but now more consistently focused and controlled. In his short tales Melville, in a sense, harnessed the declamatory pyrotechnics of *Mardi*, *Moby-Dick*, and *Pierre*, carefully releasing his imaginative energies through, and around, a collection of ironic personae. Thus Melville anticipates the twentieth century and the vogue of ironic narrator-heroes like Prufrock, Meursault, and Jake Barnes: the "real" stories that he tells, more often than not, are about his narrators' anxieties and insecurities, or their failures of vision—sometimes comically rendered, sometimes pathetically or even tragically revealed.

In eleven out of his sixteen periodical tales and sketches Melville uses first-person narrators who are in effect, if not in actuality, the protagonists in the stories they relate; yet, to varying degrees, each is an unreliable commentator on his own firsthand experiences. In the other five stories Melville experiments with aesthetic distance. Authorial privilege in "Benito Cereno" is for the most part limited to Delano's mind, although the author permits himself occasional ironic intrusions. In

"Poor Man's Pudding and Rich Man's Crumbs," "The Happy Failure," and "The Encantadas" he uses his narrators more as observers or commentators than as dramatized characters, whereas "The Bell-Tower" features a limited-omniscient narrator through whom Melville tells only "part of the story," so to speak. The intellectual, perceptual, or psychological inadequacies of Melville's first-person narrators, and their imperfect understanding of themselves, make their stories complex. At the same time these characters, like Tommo, Redburn, and Ishmael, come to life as identifiably "real" people because of their human limitations. In addition, there is the familiar Melvillean paradox that complicates the problem of what his narrators can know and, therefore, of what the reader can learn from them. As Fogle puts it, Melville's purpose in his short fiction is no different from what it was in his novels: to probe as deeply as possible into our world's "metaphysical, theological, moral, psychological, and social truths." Yet in all of Melville's short tales, the narrative protagonist as seeker for these truths is, ironically, "pitted against a finally inscrutable reality."[10]

In using the first-person technique Melville was also continuing to capitalize, as he had in the novels, on the appeal of the oral tradition of storytelling. Following Fielding's example, or the contemporary "sketchers," Lamb, Irving, and Hawthorne, Melville in his short fiction sought a "genial" relationship with his readers, to suit both the literary conventions of the familiar essay as well as his own instinctive style. He already had six expository first-person novels on the shelf in 1853, and the failure of his only omniscient-narrative attempt, *Pierre*, was growing more apparent all the time. Furthermore, as Berthoff reminds us, Melville's first-person narration gives him several literary advantages. "It allows for (though it does not automatically justify) an exploratory looseness and variety in organization and an easy freedom of inclusion; the binding and verifying personal presence of the speaker gives

10. *Melville's Shorter Tales*, pp. 4, 5.

margin, and opportunity, for that casual digressiveness which in support of a strong theme can help to secure the illusion of natural life and truth."[11]

The essential narrative persona in Melville's first six novels is the Ishmaelian "bachelor," a youthful, initially naive and uncommitted rover who ventures out into the world in quest of experience, shares his insights or his puzzlement with the reader, and, as we have seen, at times pauses in his yarn-spinning to portray his own actions or attitudes ironically. In the short fiction, the only Ishmaelian sea rover *qua* rover is the metaphysics-prone guide figure in "The Encantadas," though he is not a dramatized character. In the other first-person stories one finds in Ishmael's place a considerable variety of more "domesticated" narrative protagonists,[12] each of whom, as the next several chapters will demonstrate, has differing intellectual and psychological attributes and varying rhetorical functions that the reader must carefully evaluate. Indeed, the rhetoric of the short stories is by design more demanding than that of the novels. Melville's short fiction narrators may laugh at themselves for their impulsive or occasionally immature behavior, but they are typically less aware than were the earlier narrators—including Ishmael—of their limitations in judgment or knowledge. Thus, in the short fiction, it is the reader's task to make the final discrimination among a narrator's values and perceptions.

Melville's first story, "Bartleby," will serve well as a paradigm for his new rhetoric. The metaphysical complexities of earlier

11. *The Example of Melville*, p. 117.
12. Judith Slater, in "The Domestic Adventurer in Melville's Tales," generalizes that in six stories, "Cock-A-Doodle-Doo!" "The Lightning-Rod Man," "I and My Chimney," "Jimmy Rose," "The Apple-Tree Table," and "The Piazza," Melville transformed Ishmael into an older, less ambitious "domestic adventurer," questing closer to home now. Professor Slater notes the "common denominators" of these stories (wives, children, hearths, attics, cellars, old age) and the similar humanistic attributes of the speakers (reverence for the past, love of meditation, and a feeling of kinship with nature and divinity).

days are still there in "Bartleby"; in contrast to Ishmael's problematical questioning of man and nature, however, the narrator does not begin to see, much less to hold up for his audience's observation and response, what Melville hoped the "deep" reader would appreciate: the scrivener's philosophical significance as suffering isolato in a crowded world of forms. "Bartleby" is paradigmatic in another way, too. It illustrates how Melville turned to his contemporaries for ideas about narrative strategy and theme.

II

"Bartleby" as Paradigm

"Bartleby"

Technique and biography cannot be kept entirely separate in examining "Bartleby, the Scrivener. A Story of Wall-Street" (*Putnam's*, Nov., Dec. 1853); Melville's shift to magazine-writing, however his earlier work may have prepared him for it, was largely precipitated by circumstances.[1] *Moby-Dick* and *Pierre* had not done well, and Melville seemed to lack the psychic and aesthetic energy to write another novel. But even as the negative reviews of *Pierre* were coming out, during August of 1852 Melville was discovering the literary possibilities of the Agatha material, and sharing them with Hawthorne. In October he was invited to contribute to Putnam's new magazine, and the possibility of earning income by the page seemed especially attractive. Then, in November, he visited Hawthorne and the Agatha story came up for further discussion. Additionally, and this fact has not been given special attention, Melville acquired two volumes of Irving's works in June, 1853, just before he began writing "Bartleby."[2]

1. A balanced discussion of Melville's shift to magazine-writing, which I have drawn on here, is A. W. Plumstead, "Bartleby: Melville's Venture into a New Genre," in *Melville Annual 1965, A Symposium: Bartleby the Scrivener*, ed. Howard P. Vincent (Kent, Ohio: Kent State Univ. Press, 1966), pp. 82–93.

2. On 7 June Melville was presented with two volumes of the 1840 Lea and Blanchard edition of Irving's works (Merton M. Sealts, Jr., *Melville's Reading* [Madison: Univ. of Wisconsin Press, 1966], entry 292a). Leon Howard believes that Melville turned to "Bartleby" in the middle or late summer of 1853 (*Herman Melville*, pp. 207–08).

Of these several circumstances, the most significant for my study is that two accomplished writers of short fiction were present at the birth of Melville's first magazine story. As I have suggested in the previous chapter, Melville had had several years of preparation for his new art form and would always bring his own literary predispositions to bear on it. Yet he was ever dependent upon his sources, too, from Ellis's *Polynesian Researches* to Shakespeare, in the novels; in writing his short stories he consulted Irving and Hawthorne, and with some frequency.[3] Irving's presence is chiefly felt in the narrative technique of "Bartleby" and Hawthorne's in the story's metaphysical dimensions. Also, both writers appear to have contributed considerably to Melville's method of characterization. These influences came together in a rather complex way.

The story seems to have owed its initial form and narrative design to the example of Irving. Melville had consciously or unconsciously been under Irving's influence for several years (Evert Duyckinck once felt that Melville began his career by modeling his writing on Irving's), even though he had, for rhetorical purposes, undercut Irving's significance as a writer

3. There are only two significant commentaries on possible influences of Irving on Melville's short stories. William L. Hedges has looked briefly at echoes of Irving in "The Paradise of Bachelors and the Tartarus of Maids" in *Washington Irving: An American Study, 1802–1832* (Baltimore: Johns Hopkins Press, 1965), pp. 159–60. John Seelye's "The Contemporary 'Bartleby,'" *American Transcendental Quarterly*, 7 (Summer 1970), 12–18, is a more helpful discussion of influences, and I shall refer to his essay below.

The earliest extended analysis of Melville's use of Hawthorne's short fiction was in my unpublished dissertation, "Literary Influences and Technique in Melville's Short Fiction: 1853–1856," in 1969. Edward H. Rosenberry's "Melville and His *Mosses*," *American Transcendental Quarterly*, 7 (Summer 1970), 47–51, and my own article, "The Minor Fiction of Hawthorne and Melville," *American Transcendental Quarterly*, 14 (Spring 1972), 149–52, explore imagistic and thematic borrowings from Hawthorne in several of Melville's tales. Christy's unpublished dissertation, "The Shock of Recognition: A Psycho-Literary Study of Hawthorne's Influence on Melville's Short Fiction" (1970), is primarily a psychological analysis, treating only in general terms possible literary influences of Hawthorne on Melville.

in his review of the *Mosses* and in a complimentary letter on Hawthorne.[4] No New York man of letters could avoid breathing in a little of Irving with the atmosphere, and Tommo, Omoo, Redburn, and White-Jacket were all to some degree Crayonesque "sketchers" on tour. In addition, as William Hedges notes, Irving influenced *Mardi*, and there are strains of "gothic risibility" and Knickerbockerism in the "conceited" prose of Ishmael.[5]

Melville acquired the two volumes of Irving's works in the summer of 1853, and it seems likely that he was rereading Irving during the next three years. The rhetorical design and narrative strategy of several of Melville's tales parallel Irving's, and Crayon and his storytelling acquaintances are, it would appear, models for at least five of Melville's short story protagonists. It seems that Irving's example reinforced Melville's own best tendencies in first-person narration, and the new magazinist would have had reason to look to the older writer for short story ideas and form. The basic similarities between Irving's and Melville's tales are in matters of narrative perspective. Essentially, the "bachelor" is the controlling consciousness in Irving,[6] as he was in Melville's novels and would continue to

4. In "Hawthorne and His Mosses [Part II]," *Literary World*, 24 Aug. 1850, p. 146, Melville lamented Irving's lack of originality in comparison to Hawthorne's: ". . . that graceful writer, who perhaps of all Americans has received the most plaudits from his own country for his productions,—that very popular and amiable writer, however good and self-reliant in many things, perhaps owes his chief reputation to the self-acknowledged imitation of a foreign model [Goldsmith], and to the studied avoidance of all topics but smooth ones." Three years later, however, Melville would work to give the surface of his first-person tales the same kind of Irvingesque amiability and smoothness, meanwhile concealing deeper meanings below. Melville's other negative comment was in a letter to Evert Duyckinck on 12 Feb. 1851. Compared to Hawthorne, he wrote, Irving was "a grasshopper." This comment was made when Melville was still strongly under Hawthorne's personal influence, and two and a half years before he began to look around him for short fiction models.

5. *Washington Irving*, pp. 156–57.

6. My assessment of Irving's method generally follows that of Hedges in *Washington Irving*, pp. 128–63, passim.

be, with some interesting variations, in his tales. As story-teller within the framing devices of *Bracebridge Hall* and *Tales of a Traveller* (where, characteristically, a dinner-table acquaintance of Crayon's reads a manuscript or recounts an adventure first- or secondhand), or as Crayon himself in *The Sketch Book*, the bachelor-observer senses his estrangement from the world and lingers as a nonparticipant on the fringes of life. Prone to sentiment, both real and affected, and even to mild neurosis, Irving's sketchers often ironically reveal more about themselves than about the external reality they pretend to describe.

Melville, following up his instincts and earlier narrative strategies, modifies and expands the Crayonesque prototype in his magazine works. The first-person narrator acquires the rhetorical stature of an authentic protagonist who enters into the action of the sketch-become-tale rather than remaining outside, as observer or as teller of a story involving someone else. In other words, Melville deemphasizes Irving's often cumbersome framing devices and allows his narrators to tell their own stories. Compared to Irving's, his method is at once more dramatic and rhetorically demanding of the reader: it multiplies the possibilities for irony, making the narrator's moods and attitudes an emotional and intellectual grid through or around which the reader must, in Jamesian terms, "see."

These patterns are at work in "Bartleby." The lawyer-narrator is a Crayonesque sketcher who enjoys storytelling and could, if he pleased, "relate divers histories, at which good-natured gentlemen might smile, and sentimental souls might weep" (*SW*, p. 3). Conservative, and himself a senti-mentalist, the lawyer anticipates the narrative personae in several stories, "I and My Chimney," "Jimmy Rose," and "The Paradise of Bachelors." He insists on telling his reader about Bartleby, who was the "strangest" scrivener he ever saw. How-ever, in acknowledging at the outset the difficulty of the task he has set for himself, for "no materials exist, for a full and satisfactory biography of this man," the narrator hints at one of the central ironies of the story: he will never succeed in "characterizing" Bartleby. The scrivener's personality, inner drives, and sensibilities will remain relatively unknown quantities to the narrator. The lawyer's character sketch is, in effect, a series of attempts to align or harmonize his clerk with something he himself knows or can respond to, and these attempts continually fail. Although the lawyer never realizes it, the "chief character . . . to be presented" will not be Bartleby, but himself.

Aside from its general method, "Bartleby" may also owe its particular generic form to Irving. As an extended anecdote about an idiosyncratic law clerk, the story bears a resemblance to the eighteenth- and early nineteenth-century sketches of character published in the periodicals. More particularly, John Seelye suggests, Melville responded to Putnam's invitation to write magazine pieces by turning to the popular tradition of the "mysterious stranger" tale, which originated in America with Irving's "The Little Man in Black" (*Salmagundi*). Although Hawthorne and Poe also contributed to the genre prior to 1853 ("Wakefield," 1834, and "The Man of the Crowd," 1840), Seelye contends that the delineation of the various responses by villagers to Irving's silent stranger and the "tag-end" explanation of the Little Man's origins were patterns imitated in "Bartleby."[7]

There are, however, even more substantial similarities between Melville's tale and another story which Seelye ascribes, in passing, to the genre: "The Adventure of the Mysterious Stranger" in *Tales of a Traveller*. Irving's tale is related to Crayon in the first person by an Englishman, who had met the subject of his story in Venice. He was a young Italian, physically similar to Bartleby in his pallor, emaciation, and haggardness of brow, who kept to himself yet who for an unknown reason needed to be near people. To the narrator the young man appears "tormented by some strange fancy or apprehen-

---

7. "The Contemporary 'Bartleby,'" p. 13.

sion" and was afflicted with a "devouring melancholy."[8] Inexplicably, the morose Italian chooses the narrator as a companion, as Bartleby does the lawyer, but remains uncommunicative about his troubles, commenting only that he needs sympathy but cannot talk with his befriender.

The Englishman tries to reason the Italian out of his melancholia, but to no avail: he "seemed content to carry his load of misery in silence, and only sought to carry it by my side. There was a mute beseeching manner about him, as if he craved companionship as a charitable boon" (*TT*, p. 95). As the story progresses, the silent sufferer begins to have the same kind of effect upon Irving's indulgent narrator that the withdrawn scrivener would have upon Melville's "charitable" lawyer, yet neither man is capable of turning away the afflicted creature who seems to need his companionship. Observes Irving's narrator: "I felt this melancholy to be infectious. It stole over my spirits; interfered with all my gay pursuits, and gradually saddened my life; yet I could not prevail upon myself to shake off a being who seemed to hang upon me for support" (*TT*, pp. 95–96). Melville's lawyer responds similarly when he discovers that Bartleby had been sleeping in the office at night: "For the first time in my life a feeling of overpowering stinging melancholy seized me. . . . The bond of a common humanity now drew me irresistibly to gloom. A fraternal melancholy!" (*SW*, p. 23).

Irving's mysterious stranger eventually disappears. Characteristic of Mr. Knickerbocker's reliance on the story-within-a-story, however, he leaves his benefactor a manuscript which (in the next tale of a traveler) explains his history: he had murdered an unprincipled rival suitor and was fleeing the

8. *Tales of a Traveller* (New York: P. F. Collier's, 1880), pp. 90, 93. This and other works by Irving cited in my study are volumes in Collier's electrotyped reproduction of Putnam's Hudson Edition. In notes hereafter, *The Sketch Book*, *Tales of a Traveller*, and *Bracebridge Hall* will be abbreviated *SB*, *TT*, and *BH*, followed by the page reference.

authorities. For reasons that will be discussed below, Melville leaves Bartleby's story essentially untold, although he does throw an Irvingesque sop to the common reader in the form of a "sequel." Irving had helped Melville find a structure for his first magazine tale and had offered him a compelling narrative strategy to build upon. Melville saw that he could multiply the thematic and rhetorical possibilities of his tale by involving the reader psychologically in the narrator's repeated experiences with a "mysterious" stranger. As in Irving's tale, no single encounter of lawyer and clerk is sufficient to explain the enigmas of Bartleby's character, and if the narrator's vision remains incomplete, so, Melville implies, may the reader's.

While "The Adventure of the Mysterious Stranger" seems to have provided a pattern for Melville to follow, Bartleby is a more intense and suggestive character than Irving's romantically melancholic figure; there seem to be stronger influences from another quarter. Melville claims in *The Confidence-Man* that "original" characters are usually observable "in town" (p. 204), and there is considerable evidence to suggest that Melville turned to that skeptical and taciturn friend from nearby Lenox, with whom he had just shared the Agatha story, as he composed the portrait of Bartleby. If Melville's first short story is his most compelling tale, perhaps it is because when he wrote it he was haunted by the image of Nathaniel Hawthorne and by one of Hawthorne's most powerful themes, withdrawal and isolation.

As a nay-sayer, Bartleby is philosophically reminiscent of, and perhaps to some extent based upon, those protagonists in Hawthorne's gloomier short fiction whom critics have viewed as portraits of the artist, and in whose alienation is symbolized Hawthorne's own skeptical retreat. Goodman Brown's capitulation to pessimism and despair over the human condition, Parson Hooper's incommunicative withdrawal behind his mask, and Wakefield's more impish perversity synthesize in Bartleby, another alienated hero.[9] Philosophically, in "Bartleby" and,

9. Portions of this discussion appeared in my essay, "The Minor

with varying emphases, in later stories as well, Melville seems to have confronted anew the implications of Hawthorne's perception of "blackness." In this first story, however, he defined the ultimate extension of a Hawthornean world-view: a self-willed death. Bartleby, unlike Agatha, finally capitulates to the suffering he has experienced and to his skepticism about the possibilities for human understanding and love.

In commenting upon *The House of the Seven Gables* in a letter to Hawthorne in April 1851, Melville creates an image of both the novel and its author. He writes that the book is like a "fine old chamber" in one corner of which there is "a dark little black-letter volume in golden clasps, entitled 'Hawthorne: A Problem.' "[10] Bartleby, a symbol of that "certain tragic phase of humanity" that Melville saw embodied in Hawthorne and in his fiction as well, is also "A Problem" and

Fiction of Hawthorne and Melville" (cited above). It is intriguing that the imagery associated with Bartleby parallels descriptions of another Melville character commonly taken to be a representation of Hawthorne himself: the reclusive Vine, in *Clarel*. The time differential between "Bartleby" (1853) and *Clarel* (1876) probably had no appreciable effect upon Melville's personal image of Hawthorne; the two writers had extensive contact in the early 1850's but little thereafter (only two brief encounters when Melville was traveling in England in 1856 and 1857), and it is likely that Melville's conception of his friend was fixed pretty firmly by 1853. Like the scrivener in his "hermitage" behind his screen, Clarel's taciturn and inscrutable companion Vine prefers to "keep separate," loiters "aloof . . . shrunk / In privity," and is "The Recluse" of "manner shy" (*Clarel* [New York: Hendricks House, 1960], Part I, xxviii, l. 51; xxx, ll. 82–83; xxix, title and l. 9). In his characteristic pose, staring wordlessly on the Dead Sea, Vine recalls Bartleby's familiar stance in a "dead-wall revery." Vine's first appearance in the poem, in the Sepulcher of Kings, is suggestive:

> But who is he uncovered seen,
> Profound in shadow of the tomb
> Reclined, with meditative mien
> Intent upon the tracery?
>
> (Part I, xxviii. ll. 37–40)

The image here is essentially that of Bartleby's withdrawal into death, when he is discovered lying on his side in the Tombs, his eyes still open.

10. *Letters*, p. 124.

a black-letter study. Hawthorne said "No! in thunder," and, Melville adds, "all men who say *yes*, lie"; to the same effect Bartleby states "I would prefer not to." The scrivener declines to adopt the distorted values and dehumanizing strictures of the outside world, and his soft-spoken refusal to join the ordinary course of life carries a strength of conviction equal to Hawthorne's emphatic "No!" Bartleby may speak for Hawthorne but he also speaks for mankind, and, true to his problematical nature, he whispers two different messages. Representing those who would "prefer not" to commit themselves to a meaningless way of life, he is a stoical study in what Melville terms in his story "passive resistance"; but through him Melville also warns humanity against a self-destructive surrender to a vision of blackness.

Melville may have begun his tale as a parable of his own encounters with Hawthorne and his writings, but he used with brilliant effect a sentimental "sketcher" of somewhat limited perception to broaden the psychological and symbolical dimensions of his story. For the unnamed narrator comes to represent any man who, forced at last to question the assumptions and values he has always lived by, hesitates to admit to himself and to his readers that he faces a crisis at all; who, pushed beyond the limits of his own understanding and humanity, rationalizes his failings.

The first of Melville's short fiction "bachelors," the lawyer begins his story with an Irvingesque "author's account of himself." This opening sketch serves two rhetorical functions. It reveals the lawyer to be something of a sentimentalist, interested in conveying to his reader what he believes will be poignant impressions of his own personal "involvement" in his strange scrivener's life. Secondly, and more important, the self-portrait discloses how inextricably bound up the lawyer is in the material world.

The ethic that informs the narrator's life style, and too often his judgment as well, is that of free-enterprise capitalism. However, the narrator is not an ambitious lawyer; a man of "peace," he is content to do a "snug" business among rich men's bonds and mortgages, in the "cool tranquillity" of his "snug retreat" on Wall Street. His hero, and former client, is the late John Jacob Astor, a name that, he admits with a flourish, "I love to repeat; for it hath a rounded and orbicular sound to it, and rings like unto bullion." Astor had once commended him for his "prudence" and "method," yet in bragging that his associates consider him "an eminently *safe* man," the lawyer unwittingly suggests that inside knowledge about even financially shady deals would be secure with him.

A telling sign of his prudent but always utilitarian approach to his world is the office routine itself. He is willing to indulge the idiosyncrasies of Turkey and Nippers so long as they are, at least during half of each working day, "useful" to him (*SW*, pp. 7, 8). Thus, while Bartleby continues with his copying, although he may "prefer not" to follow certain orders, his employer keeps him on as a "useful" servant (*SW*, p. 17; the narrator will employ the word again when he introduces Bartleby to the "useful" grub-man in the prison). When the scrivener gives up copying, however, and his uselessness begins to interfere with the "method" of the lawyer's office, Bartleby constitutes a threat.

The rhythmic pattern of events prior to Bartleby's inevitable dismissal makes up the story's essential form: from the introductory self-portrait to the page-long "sequel" concerning the scrivener's earlier work in the Dead Letter Office occur approximately a dozen confrontations between the employer and his clerk. Melville's structure is rhetorically quite effective. It enables him to exhibit several distinctive responses to the enigma of Bartleby, none of which succeeds in revealing his character. Thus the levels of available meaning are multiplied, and the reader is left free to identify with any, or none, of the lawyer's emotional and mental reactions to his scrivener. Melville would find this method useful later, in the encounters of narrators and "original" characters in "The Fiddler," "The Lightning-Rod Man," and "Benito Cereno," for example.

Melville's rhetorical strategy dictates that no interpretation of Bartleby offered by the lawyer could ever be complete, for the scrivener is a phenomenon totally alien to the narrator's experience and sensibilities. Yet the story raises an even larger rhetorical question. The lawyer may have his limitations, but does not Melville also suggest that Bartleby is incapable of giving enough of his own self to deserve even that charity which his employer extends? Where does the moral or ethical emphasis of the tale rest, finally? In the best Ishmaelian tradition, Melville offers no neat answers.

Among his dozen or so confrontations with the scrivener, six of the lawyer's encounters are crucial in terms of method and meaning. Melville seeks at the initial stage of employer-employee interaction to identify the reader with the lawyer's perspective, for purposes of immediacy and verisimilitude; quickly, however, Melville tests the reader-narrator relationship by skewing the lawyer's angle of perception.

Thus, at Bartleby's first preference not to perform some routine clerical tasks, the narrator is portrayed as baffled and stunned, as almost anyone would be (*SW*, pp. 13–16). With the second round of Bartleby's preference-stating, however, a measurable amount of separation takes place between lawyer and reader. The lawyer decides, with a certain logic but with a recognizable degree of self-congratulation, that because Bartleby is "useful" to him he should befriend his clerk; in so doing he could "purchase a delicious self-approval" for his conscience (*SW*, p. 17). The lawyer's studied self-righteousness gives way to what he claims to be a disturbing if not a painful awareness of Bartleby's spiritual condition, in the third phase of the encounters. He is surprised to find one Sunday that Bartleby has been sleeping in the office at night, solitary and companionless; but how authentic or sincere is the narrator's recounting of his discovery?

Immediately then the thought came sweeping across me, what miserable friendlessness and loneliness are here revealed! His poverty is great; but his solitude, how horrible! Think of it. Of a Sunday, Wall Street is deserted as Petra; and every night of every day it is an emptiness. This building, too, which of week-days hums with industry and life, at nightfall echoes with sheer vacancy, and all through Sunday is forlorn. And here Bartleby makes his home; sole spectator of a solitude which he has seen all populous—a sort of innocent and transformed Marius brooding among the ruins of Carthage! (*SW*, pp. 22–23)

The lawyer has a felicitous turn of phrase, but his effusiveness is over-elegant and melodramatic—more appropriate to a romantic sketcher of "fine sentiments," trying to appeal to his audience, than to a sensitive perceiver of human need.

"A fraternal melancholy!" exclaims the lawyer as he contemplates Bartleby's loneliness. "For both I and Bartleby were sons of Adam." Just as the reader is beginning to ask how much real communion there is in a fit of sympathetic melancholia, the narrator's mood passes. When he recalls forlorn Bartleby's "pallid haughtiness" and his habit of staring incommunicatively upon the dead brick wall outside his window, the lawyer feels "melancholy merge into fear" and "pity into repulsion." In attempting to account for this shift the protagonist says, defensively, "They err who would assert that invariably this is owing to the inherent selfishness of the human heart." After all, "it was his soul that suffered, and his soul I could not reach" (*SW*, pp. 24–25). Of course this is precisely the point; the lawyer seeks on the next morning to "reach" Bartleby's soul in a common-sense fashion—by asking him questions about himself—failing to understand that an uncommon Bartleby who prefers to say nothing about himself cannot be so easily plumbed.

In the fourth confrontation (*SW*, pp. 27–28), the lawyer's rational analysis of his clerk's behavior and its effects reinforces what his emotional responses had told him. He realizes that both he and his other assistants have, unconsciously, got in the habit of using the word "prefer," and he knows now that he must surely dismiss this "demented man" who is affecting them all in a "mental way." The scrivener's decision to do no more copying provides the lawyer his excuse, and he gives Bartleby six days to leave.

Up to this point Melville has portrayed his enigmatic scrivener from a narrative perspective that has undergone several reorientations. Initially, the lawyer is simply perplexed by Bartleby's behavior, nothing more; then he looks at his clerk from the standpoint of self-righteousness, again as would a self-styled victim of melancholia, and yet again as a utilitarian rationalist. These four stances do not assist in revealing the "true" Bartleby to the lawyer, nor are they meant to; Bartleby is simply not going to make himself available for revelation.

In the fifth confrontation the scrivener undergoes metaphysical analysis, although the metaphysics is only rhetorical tomfoolery on Melville's part. From behind the persona of his narrator he toys with the reader for two full pages using a very large pun on the Doctrine of the Assumption, the Catholic belief that the Virgin Mary ascended into Heaven on August 15.[11] Having given Bartleby severance pay, the lawyer assumes that he would now leave. "I *assumed* the ground that depart he must," recollects the lawyer, "and upon that assumption built all I had to say." But the narrator is "thunderstruck" six days later to find Bartleby still there. Characteristically, his response is melodramatic and exaggerated: ". . . I stood like the man who, pipe in mouth, was killed one cloudless afternoon long ago in Virginia, by summer lightning; at his own warm open window he was killed, and remained leaning out there upon the dreamy afternoon, till some one touched him, when he fell." Melville's punning on the Assumption grows explicit:

What was to be done? or, if nothing could be done, was there anything further that I could *assume* in the matter?

11. I am indebted to Professor Jerry Gerber of Duke University for pointing out this pun to me.

Yes, as before I had prospectively assumed that Bartleby would depart, so now I might retrospectively assume that departed he was. . . . I might enter my office in a great hurry, and pretending not to see Bartleby at all, walk straight against him as if he were air. . . . It was hardly possible that Bartleby could withstand such an application of the doctrine of assumptions. But upon second thoughts the success of the plan seemed rather dubious. (*SW*, pp. 32–33)

Dubious indeed, for Bartleby is Bartleby, not the risen Virgin Mary. Further along, Melville makes one last punning reference to the metaphysical question of Bartleby's power to transcend this mortal sphere. Still baffled by the clerk's continuing presence in the office, the lawyer demands: "What earthly right have you to stay here?"

Melville's pun on the Assumption is but one of several *jeux-de-mots* and witty asides in "Bartleby." The humorous dimensions of the story are an essential part of its surprising fullness and complexity of texture; the reader enjoys the Dickensian idiosyncrasies of Turkey and Nippers and laughs at the narrator for his sentimentality and propensity to over-dramatize his own plight, but the humor ceases when Bartleby's fate begins to close in on him.[12]

12. Two substantive revisions in the *Putnam's* version of the story for the collected *Piazza Tales* help to intensify its power. In the first change, "Bartleby, the Scrivener. A Story of Wall-Street" becomes simply "Bartleby"; apparently Melville was willing to sacrifice the pun on "wall" in favor of the increase in poignancy or emotional force afforded by the shortened title. The second revision eliminates a humorous distraction from the compelling final pages of the tale. In *Putnam's*, "Mr. Cutlets," the grub-man at the prison, invites Bartleby to dine with him and Mrs. Cutlets in her "private room." For *The Piazza Tales* the cook's proper name and the invitation are dropped, and the grub-man merely asks Bartleby what he will have for dinner. In both versions of the story the scrivener's reply is identical, and it conveys a universe of meaning: " 'I prefer not to dine to-day,' said Bartleby, turning away. 'It would disagree with me; I am unused to dinners.' So saying, he slowly moved to the other side of the inclosure, and took up a position fronting the dead-wall" (*SW*, p. 44).

The last important confrontation between lawyer and clerk raises the moral and theological questions that Melville was most concerned with in his story. Angry that the scrivener has achieved a "cadaverous triumph" over him, the lawyer is just barely able to contain what he now finds to be almost murderous thoughts about Bartleby. Luckily, he acts in accordance with his previously advertised virtue of prudence, and he recalls the charitable commandment "that ye love one another." Comforting himself during the next few days by reading "Edwards on the Will" and "Priestley on Necessity," he is nearly convinced that "Bartleby was billeted upon me for some mysterious purpose of an all-wise Providence, which it was not for a mere mortal like me to fathom" (SW, p. 35). But the narrator's Christian charity and faith capitulate to human pride and a slightly paranoid imbalance. His professional acquaintances criticize him for retaining in his chambers an odd vagrant who does absolutely no work, and the lawyer's imagination—more neurotic than melodramatic now—projects a lurid scene:

And as the idea came upon me of [Bartleby's] possibly turning out a long-lived man, and keep occupying my chambers, and denying my authority; and perplexing my visitors; and scandalizing my professional reputation; and casting a general gloom over the premises; keeping soul and body together to the last upon his savings (for doubtless he spent but half a dime a day), and in the end perhaps outlive me, and claim possession of my office by right of his perpetual occupancy: as all these dark anticipations crowded upon me more and more . . . a great change was wrought in me. I resolved to gather all my faculties together, and forever rid me of this intolerable incubus. (SW, pp. 36–37)

Yet his mood would shift again. The dismayed narrator is still essentially a "man of peace" (SW, p. 6), incapable of physically ejecting Bartleby and hesitant to summon the police. Instead, he moves his entire office elsewhere, and, "strange to say—I tore myself from him whom I had so longed to be rid of" (*SW*, p. 38).

The lawyer is baffled by his scrivener because he is conditioned by the method of his profession and his life. Although one faults the protagonist for his blindness, Bartleby might, after all, have affected anyone as he did the narrator. One critic contends that the lawyer cannot "involve himself emotionally" in the isolation of Bartleby, because the effort would entail "too great a strain upon his capacity for love and pity."[13] And so, perhaps, with the reader. However, the lawyer's post-separation guilt and uncertainty about his lack of meaningful involvement only reinforce our image of his ineffectuality. Able to put up with occasional troublesome quirks in his office workers so long as they perform their duties, the lawyer fails when the humane indulgences that Bartleby seemed to seek grow too taxing. When his former landlord sends word that he must do something about the man he abandoned, the frustrated lawyer literally denies his scrivener thrice—in effect betraying him into the hands of the authorities.[14] His denials make him feel guilty, but his eleventh-hour efforts at the prison to provide for his clerk, his offers of lodging and a job and his paying for meals that Bartleby prefers not to eat, come too late. In his three most emphatic and resolute statements Bartleby tells his onetime employer, "I know you," "I want nothing to say to you," and "I know where I am" (*SW*, p. 43).

As a "reward" for his puzzled readers and as a gesture by which he hopes to clear himself of any accusations of irresponsibility and uncharitableness towards Bartleby, the lawyer

13. William Bysshe Stein, "Melville's Comedy of Faith," *ELH*, 27 (Dec. 1960), 319.

14. Several critics have noted that Bartleby is a Christ-figure and that the lawyer's tale contains various Christian images and allusions. See particularly Chapter V, "Worldly Safety and Other-worldly Saviors," in H. Bruce Franklin, *The Wake of the Gods: Melville's Mythology* (Stanford: Stanford Univ. Press, 1963), and Donald M. Fiene, "Bartleby the Christ," *American Transcendental Quarterly*, 7 (Summer 1970), 18–23.

passes along "one little item of rumor" as a possible explanation of his scrivener's strange personality. Bartleby's experiences in the Washington Dead Letter Office had apparently convinced him that all life held was deprivation and despair—thus his pitiable forlornness.

Yet Melville would not so easily explain away the scrivener, nor so readily pardon the narrator. Surely there are more significant meanings latent in Bartleby's insistent use of the word "prefer" and in the walls he seems to identify with. During one of their encounters the narrator tested the extent of his scrivener's perversity by asking him to run an errand to the Post Office (probably the last place, if the rumor is correct, that Bartleby would ever want to go). The scrivener gives his standard reply, "I would prefer not to." "You *will* not?" demands the lawyer; "I *prefer* not," answers Bartleby (italics Melville's; *SW*, p. 19). The lawyer, characteristically, offers no meaningful interpretive commentary on this crucial distinction, but for the modern reader the sequence is an intriguing prefiguration of the existential dilemma. In "Bartleby" Melville portrays not only an obsessive Hawthornean vision of blackness, but also an image of one man's confrontation with what he feels to be the meaninglessness of the universe. Ahab had spoken of an "unreasoning force," inexorably in control of all nature, that denies man both identity and power. There is no possibility of meaningful action, Bartleby seems to say, and it is certain that man cannot successfully will anything. Perhaps the only tenable stance is merely to *prefer* to do something; this gives one at least a temporary hedge against fate, and somehow it is not quite so painful if one's "preferences" are denied. Bartleby never says "I *will* not," and the lawyer, habitually an avoider of conflicts and a postponer of decisions until his "leisure," never pushes his clerk beyond his preferences. At one point in the story the lawyer explains how difficult it was for him to put up with all those "peculiarities, privileges, and unheard-of exemptions" of Bartleby's, failing to realize that the "exemptions" Bartleby enjoyed were not of the clerk's making, but of his own.

Melville suggests that all man can choose to do is to endure and to state his wishes, although there are always hazards in making an obsession out of preferring. For if the lawyer errs in judgment, so does Bartleby in preferring to attach himself to one whom he, for some reason, has chosen to be his companion in his isolation ("I would prefer *not* to quit you," the scrivener tells his employer late in the story). Does Bartleby, the almost catatonic isolato who seems deathly afraid of even being brushed against by a fellow clerk, have the right to expect comfort or companionship from a person with whom he is incapable of sharing even the smallest modicum of his inner self? Unlike Ahab, Bartleby has neither strength nor will to aggress through the walls which hedge him in, a prisoner, and the lawyer's desertion is for the clerk like the final turning of the key in the lock. Indeed, Bartleby seems voluntarily to have made himself a prisoner of the walls he sees, perhaps because they, alone, do not make any demands on his privacy.[15]

15. (I am grateful to Rebecca Chalker, a former student, for this perspective.) Bartleby's movement in the story is primarily from the four walls of the law office to the four walls of the city prison; here, in his final confrontation with the barriers that society erects, he dies. Yet within the office walls, which demarcate Bartleby's world of temporary endurance, Melville proliferates his motif—perhaps to the point of unnecessary ambiguity. One window of the office looks out upon a white skylight shaft, another upon a tall brick wall, "black by age," and Bartleby's upon a "dead" brick wall only three feet away. The scrivener's green screen suggests something eternal in his nature or significance, especially when the greenness of the enclosed grass-plot receives emphasis in the prison scene, and his "dead" wall is symbolic. But what meanings are attached to the other colors, white and black? Also, the outer walls of the lawyer's chamber and the prison walls are permanent, fixed (like Bartleby); the inner walls of the office are moveable, but to what purpose, exactly? Leo Marx, in "Melville's Parable of the Walls," *Sewanee Review*, 61 (Autumn 1953), 602–27, reads the story as a parable of the artist and sees some relationship between the inner, folding walls and the theme of human manipulation (the lawyer can wall off his clerks as he chooses). It is also significant, I

The scrivener, suggests Henry Murray, used silence and immobility to defend his integrity, but in the process he became alienated and a misanthrope.[16] Thus, he dies alone and in a manner appropriate to his fundamental preference to remain separate: he prefers, finally, not to eat and dies with his head resting on the cold prison stones, rather than on humanity's pillow.

"Bartleby" and Technique in the Magazine Tales

As Melville experimented with aesthetic distance and narrative form in his magazine fiction he returned frequently to two basic narrative personae: that of the genial, sentimental anecdotist who enjoys painting sketches of character or social settings, or writing familiar essays about himself, and that of the ironic protagonist who, in a sense, becomes the victim of his own story. Works in the first category include "Jimmy Rose" and "I and My Chimney," while "The Fiddler" and "Cock-A-Doodle-Doo!" feature the second type of narrative pose. "Bartleby" is paradigmatically significant because it illustrates both basic narrative postures: the lawyer is genial and an engaging anecdotist, but he is at the same time an ironic figure of incomplete perceptions. None of Melville's stories is free of rhetorical irony, and hence, as "Bartleby" would suggest, one should not force distinctions between "sentimental" narrative and "ironic" narrative too far. Chapters three and four, therefore, will examine shades of Melvillean irony in artistically related stories that feature the two dominant modes I have outlined here. Chapters five through eight will discuss Melville's continuing experimentation in his short tales with the complex relationships among narrative form, epistemology, and vision.

---

would suggest, that the lawyer, no less than Bartleby, needs walls around him to ensure his "safe" existence in his "snug" retreat on Wall Street.

16. "Bartleby and I," in *Melville Annual 1965*, pp. 3–24, passim.

III

Irony in the Sentimental Mode

"Jimmy Rose"

"Jimmy Rose" (*Harper's*, Nov. 1855) bears a certain structural resemblance to "Bartleby." It, too, is a character sketch in the form of a familiar essay; the narrator, William Ford, spends several pages describing his own surroundings and chatting about his likes and dislikes before he introduces his announced subject, the "gentle Jimmy Rose." Melville's point is, again, that Ford, like the lawyer in "Bartleby," is in many ways the real subject of his own sketch. Philosophically, "Jimmy Rose" is a minor work, but rhetorically the story is a carefully rendered satire on the limits of human perception and self-knowledge.

As a piece of sentiment, "Jimmy Rose" owes a good deal to Irving's "Little Britain," in *The Sketch Book*. Both works, first of all, are gently ironic self-portraits of narrators who are nostalgic for the "good old days." Each is reluctant to accept the values of competition and the work ethic, and each is slow to adjust to the ever accelerating changes taking place in the modern world. The two sketches are essentially lamentations that the "antiquated folks and fashions" and "good old . . . manners" (Irving's phrases) have fallen by the way because of the debilitating effects of economic and social change.

Crayon had for many years lived in a small district of "very venerable" but now deteriorating houses in the center of London, where once the Dukes of Brittany resided. Unhappily, as London grew, "rank and fashion rolled off to the west, and trade creeping on at their heels took possession of their de-

45

serted abodes" (*SB*, p. 339). Melville's character sketch begins as Irving's does: the narrator for several years had been making his home in an old ward of New York City, in a quaintly but richly furnished house formerly owned by a onetime millionaire, Jimmy Rose. Both Rose and this part of the city had, however, fallen into social decline as a result of economic change: "once the haunt of style and fashion, full of gay parlors and bridal chambers," the old district was now "transformed into counting-rooms and warehouses. These bales and boxes usurp the place of sofas; day-books and ledgers are spread where once the delicious breakfast toast was buttered" (*SW*, p. 241).

Despite the effects of time and change, both writers note, the process of transformation is fortunately not complete, for "Little Britain still bears traces of its former splendor," and in old New York "some monument[s] of departed days survived." Then follows a catalog of the still-elegant interiors of the mansions where the two narrators reside; in both works the reader is asked to look indulgently, if not reverently, at the grotesquely carved doorways and mantels, fretted ceilings, ornate cornices, panelled wainscots, and other furbishings typical of the previous century. Having created a sense of place and a feeling for the old styles, both narrators also sketch in profiles of the folk who still live in the two districts, meanwhile pointing out the similarities between themselves and these older inhabitants and affirming the values and traditions of the old times.

As a character sketch of a wealthy man whom fortune turned against, Melville's story is a particularized study of the economic perils of modern times, whereas Irving's is a more panoramic commentary on the rise and fall of a whole district. Despite the difference in scope, Irving's sketch apparently suggested a narrative design for Melville, while it gave him a rich thematic pattern to work with. Irving may even have planted the seed in Melville's imagination which would yield the central imagery, if not the central figure, in his sketch. A few lines of poetry scratched on Crayon's window-glass by a former inhabitant extolled the "charms" of "many a beauty of Little Britain, who has long, long since bloomed, faded, and passed away." And so the blooming roses in the cheek of charming Jimmy Rose faded, at last, in death, although Melville's narrator hopes that "[t]ransplanted to another soil" Jimmy's roses "may immortally survive!" (*SW*, p. 253).

Paralleling his technique in "Agatha," Melville uses imagery in his story to help develop character and meaning. Jimmy's introduction comes at the end of a page-long rhapsody on the faded rose- and peacock-patterned Louis XVI wallpaper in the Fords' parlor—a room which the sentimental and old-fashioned narrator refuses to let his wife and daughters remodel. He loves to dwell upon the "real elegance," albeit rather dimmed, and the "sweet engaging pensiveness" of the peacocks in the room, but chiefly he associates the parlor with Jimmy Rose. From this point on the tale has a twofold development: as Ford entrenches himself in memories of Jimmy's social success and abrupt decline and reminds the reader that through it all Jimmy's carmine cheeks never lost their glow, he not only succeeds in evoking Jimmy himself but also reveals his own attraction for the gilt-edged showiness and social artificialities of the past.[1]

Over the years the narrator has come to identify himself with Jimmy Rose. He is envious of Jimmy's flair for saying fine things finely, still loves to repeat the millionaire's stylized banquet toasts (even though acknowledging that Rose plagiarized them), and recalls Jimmy's charming sway over the female sex. Along with the social graces, Ford also celebrates the material trappings of Jimmy's domain, as in the following passage in which he fondly balances Jimmy's charm and effervescence with his physical furnishings: "His uncommon cheeriness; the splendor of his dress; his sparkling wit; radiant

1. As James W. Gargano puts it, "Jimmy Rose" is in some ways "a period piece that disparages the period." See "Melville's 'Jimmy Rose,'" *Western Humanities Review*, 16 (Summer 1962), 279.

chandeliers; infinite fund of small-talk; French furniture; glowing welcomes to his guests; his bounteous heart and board; his noble graces and his glorious wine; what wonder if all these drew crowds to Jimmy's hospitable abode?" (*SW*, p. 244). And what wonder that the narrator was among these crowds, for he liked grandeur and show as much as Jimmy did.

The narrator's repeated apostrophe to Jimmy, "Ah, poor, poor Jimmy—God guard us all—poor Jimmy Rose!" pulses like a sentimental heartthrob throughout the story, and by the end of the piece the narrator, as he speaks of his own tears, seems to pity himself almost as much as he does Jimmy. Yet Ford's departed hero was, after all, a shallow figure who turned not to work but to charity when his finances collapsed.[2] In another passage, the narrator comes as close as he ever will to admitting the truth about his over-elegant friend:

> Neither did Jimmy give up his courtly ways [as he trudged about town for charitable tea and cakes]. Whenever there were ladies at the table, sure were they of some fine word; though, indeed, toward the close of Jimmy's life, the young ladies rather thought his compliments somewhat musty, smacking of cocked hats and small-clothes— nay, of old pawnbrokers' shoulder-lace and sword belts. For there still lingered in Jimmy's address a subdued sort of martial air; he having in his palmy days been . . . a general of the State militia. . . . Is it that this military leaning in a man of unmilitary heart—that is, a gentle, peaceable heart—is an indication of some weak love of vain display? But ten to one it is not so. (*SW*, p. 251)

Jimmy *was* vain and artificial, but Ford could not let himself admit it. To do so would mean to acknowledge the shallowness in his own character and his reluctance, if not inability, to adjust to the modern world.

2. Slater, in "The Domestic Adventurer in Melville's Tales," p. 274, also points out that the narrator's perceptions about Jimmy have become "clouded" over the years.

"I and My Chimney"

The chatty, informal narrator of "I and My Chimney" (*Putnam's*, March 1856) is another of Melville's genial sentimentalists. Like Ford in "Jimmy Rose," he is restless in a marriage to a youthful wife who is impatient with his idiosyncrasies, he worships the past, and he defends his old age and old-fashioned tastes with a stubborn, if not at times a blind, tenacity. As a contemporary of Melville's observed, "I and My Chimney" is "thoroughly magazinish." The humorous interplay between husband and wife is appealing in its own right, yet Melville's ribald punning, as well as the suggestive symbolic and psychological overtones of the story, have made the tale something of a cause célèbre among Melville readers.

"I and My Chimney" owes its vitality and charm, and much of its symbolic import, to Melville's success in synthesizing ideas and patterns from at least three different sources: his own experiences, some motifs in Irving, and Hawthorne's sketch "Fire Worship." Merton Sealts has discussed at some length the ways in which Melville's personal history informs his story, and only a brief recapitulation is needed here.[3] There are strong parallels between the narrator's concern for the health of his chimney and Melville's anxiety about his own condition in 1852–53. Both the author and his family were apprehensive about the possibility of mental derangement, and Oliver Wendell Holmes was called in—ostensibly for consultation about Melville's troubles with sciatica. The architect summoned to consider removing the chimney, Scribe ("writer"), may represent Holmes himself, and the assertive, enterprising, and unsympathetic wife in the tale is said to be modeled on Melville's mother, who was known to be energetic, industrious, and occasionally critical.

Irving's "Rip Van Winkle" seems also to have had an effect on "I and My Chimney." Both works develop the conflict

3. "Herman Melville's 'I and My Chimney,'" *American Literature*, 13 (May 1941), 142–54.

between the old and the new, as had "Little Britain" and "Jimmy Rose." In "Rip Van Winkle" and "I and My Chimney," however, Irving and Melville give psychological vitality to the conflict by pitting, archetypally, a youthful, energetic, and shrewish wife against her older, indolent, but likable husband, one who would have been far happier as a bachelor and who, therefore, seeks solace in bachelor pursuits. The patterns synthesize with neat irony in "Rip Van Winkle." Rip retreats to the Catskills and is finally freed from his termagant wife, although he must pay a price for his escape: the nervousness and bustle of post-Revolutionary America disconcert him, and for a while he thinks he would have been better off in the old days, after all.

The stodgy old narrator of "I and My Chimney" is in a similar retreat before a predatory wife, but, unlike Rip, he barricades himself for the siege rather than seeking an escape. His young wife subscribes to the ladies' magazines for the latest fashions, keeps up with Swedenborgianism and spirit-rapping, and "always buys her new almanac a month before the new year." Furthermore she is a "natural projector. The maxim, 'Whatever is, is right,' is not hers. Her maxim is, Whatever is, is wrong; and what is more, must be altered; and what is still more, must be altered right away. Dreadful maxim for the wife of a dozy old dreamer like me, who . . . will . . . go out of my road a quarter of a mile, to avoid the sight of a man at work" (*SW*, p. 385). Contrary to his wife, who "doesn't believe in old age," the narrator prefers oldness: "For that cause mainly loving old Montaigne, and old cheese, and old wine; and eschewing young people . . . new books, and early potatoes, and very fond of my old claw-footed chair, and . . . my betwisted old grape-vine . . . and . . . high above all, am fond of my high-mantled old chimney" (*SW*, p. 386).

In developing the conflict between the old and the new, there is no doubt that Irving and Melville identified considerably with their protagonists' respect for the past. Both authors stressed the permanence of the past, hoping that the values of the old times could prove a buffer to the fragmenting, if not emasculating, forces of the present. Furthermore, Irving's images of eternally beautiful mountains and glens and Melville's emphasis on old cheese, an old grape-vine, and especially on the vitality of the old chimney, underscore the organic qualities of the past sadly lacking in the hurried mechanical motions of modern times—and in the impatient activities of aggressive wives. In his late unpublished essay, "Rip Van Winkle's Lilac," Melville finds another image of the past: an ever-youthful lilac tree appropriately symbolizes the presence of the past and Rip's refusal to sacrifice his identity to new world changes.

Irving may have helped Melville focus thematic ideas in "I and My Chimney," but Hawthorne seems to have inspired his central symbol. Edward Rosenberry[4] traces the motif of the hearth as sacred and the general theme of defending it from attack to Hawthorne's sentimental essay "Fire Worship" (which Melville had praised in his review of *Mosses from an Old Manse*).[5] A closer analysis of the two works turns up additional parallels in rhetorical structure (schemes to replace the faithful hearth are recounted in detail) and in imagery associated with the hearth (both authors, for example, praise the fireplace as "sociable," as having a "warm heart," and as promoting brotherhood). Hawthorne's essay, however, remains a nostalgic apostrophe to the hearth, slight in comparison to the complexities of Melville's tale. The "elemental spirit" typifying "the picturesque, the poetic, and the beautiful" only

4. "Melville and His *Mosses*," pp. 47–51, passim.
5. "Fire Worship" was first published in the *Democratic Review*, Dec. 1843, and later collected in *Mosses from an Old Manse* (1846). Quotations from this essay will be from the Houghton-Mifflin edition (Boston, 1882). In "Hawthorne and His Mosses [Part I]," *Literary World*, 17 Aug. 1850, p. 125, Melville lauded a passage from "Fire Worship" that celebrated the "domestic kindness" of the fireplace, a benevolent quality all the more "sweet" when one contemplates the fire's potential for destruction. Portions of my discussion of Hawthorne's influence on Melville's story appeared in my essay, "The Minor Fiction of Hawthorne and Melville."

flickers abstractly in Hawthorne's hearth, whereas Melville's solidly real chimney stands assertively for the narrator's ego and Job-like integrity. For Hawthorne the fireplace is a vaguely metaphoric "beacon light of humanity"; for Melville the chimney *is* humanity, in its eternal struggle for self-preservation. Yet at the same time the chimney is a great source of humor and good fun.

Melville's digressive and improvisatory mode keeps "I and My Chimney" in constant motion, and as a stylistic and verbal performance it is equal to anything in the Melville canon. In punning on the chimney's shape and size, the surgical operations it has undergone, and its position relative to the narrator, to say nothing of its power to hatch the wife's eggs, Melville toys with his nineteenth-century audience even more boldly than he had in describing Carlo's "hand-organ" in *Redburn*, or the whale's "grandissimus" in *Moby-Dick*. However, Melville's puns operate on a serious level, too. The wife's repeated endeavors to replace the grotesquely phallic chimney with a yonic entrance hall of "generous amplitude" threaten both the "foundation" of the house, and the old narrator's fundamental self, both physical and spiritual. So far as he is concerned, the narrator calmly explains to his wife, the chimney remains a "sober, substantial fact," incapable of replacement (*SW*, p. 384). But to the reader he reveals that the chimney is also his only "masculine prerogative" that has not yet fallen to his aggressive, indeed almost voracious, wife.

The chimney, like the whale, is a seemingly endless source of anecdote, as well as meaning. Following up his instincts in narrative portraiture, Melville develops in his tale the comic possibilities of human reflexes and involuntary gesture, as characters react to the chimney or are affected by it. For example, the narrator often finds himself in his cellar, pondering the fabulous dimensions of his chimney and wondering about its age and origins. One day he is so "penetrated with wonder" by the chimney's "druidical look" and its seeming connection with primeval nature that he unconsciously gets a spade from the garden and begins to dig around its base: "I was a little out of my mind, I now think . . . [and] obscurely prompted by dreams of striking upon some old, earthen-worn memorial of that by-gone day when, into all this gloom, the light of heaven entered, as the masons laid the foundation-stones" (*SW*, p. 380). The scene turns, comically and dramatically, upon the narrator's embarrassment at being discovered at his work by a neighbor, who had entered unobserved:

> "Gold digging, sir?"
> "Nay, sir," answered I, starting, "I was merely—ahem! —merely—I say I was merely digging—round my chimney."
> "Ah, loosening the soil, to make it grow. Your chimney, sir, you regard as too small, I suppose. . . ." (*SW*, p. 381)

Another episode involves "a certain stylish young gentleman, a great exquisite," who had come to call on one of the narrator's daughters. He passed the evening with Anna in the dining room, which was a chamber peculiarly affected by the chimney's location at the center of the house. The rooms downstairs were connected to each other, since there could be no central hallway, and the dining room had no less than nine doors, "opening in all directions, and into all sorts of places." The elegant young man stayed late, and

> after abundance of superfine discourse, all the while retaining his hat and cane, made his profuse adieus, and with repeated graceful bows proceeded to depart, after the fashion of courtiers from the Queen, and by so doing, opening a door at random, with one hand placed behind, very effectually succeeded in backing himself into a dark pantry, where he carefully shut himself up, wondering [sic] there was no light in the entry. (*SW*, p. 390)

"After several strange noises as of a cat among the crockery," the narrator continues, "he reappeared through the same door looking uncommonly crest-fallen" and, "with a deeply embarrassed air," asked Anna for directions. The young man was gratifyingly matter-of-fact and unaffected thereafter. Indeed, he was "more candid than ever," Melville quips, "having inadvertently thrust his white kids into an open drawer of Havana sugar, under the impression, probably, that being what they call 'a sweet fellow,' his route might possibly lie in that direction."

Amidst the punning and the comic anecdotes, the narrator's chimney assumes important philosophical dimensions in the story. In making proud claims for his chimney's impressiveness as the "grand seignior" and "king" in the house, and for its massiveness and majesty, as well as its mystery, the narrator is romantically celebrating himself. By worshipping the chimney, serving it, sentimentally communing with it, and defending it from harassment and possible destruction, he is simultaneously preserving his own identity. And yet the chimney represents more than the protagonist's own personality. It becomes a complex symbol for humanity as a whole—man's spirit, his inviolable soul, his masculinity, as well as his stubborn egotism and whimsical idiosyncrasies.

Melville's choice as narrator of a likable old hearty who has a penchant for sentiment and for philosophy also helps to expand the implications of the story. The protagonist's "indolent" habit of meditation, as he and his chimney "smoke and philosophize together," makes the expository form of the story appear natural. Finally, the narrator's digressions on old age, integrity, and man's quest for identity and fulfillment convey the tragicomic nature of life itself.

IV

Experiments in Rhetorical Irony

By virtue of his rhetorical method, Melville's first-person narrators, in novels and stories alike, are usually more acted upon than acting. By the same token, meaning in a Melville work seems to dwell outside the narrator, rather than to be projected by him onto the fictional landscape. Thus Melville's writings are "realistic" pieces of romance. Narrators like the lawyer in "Bartleby" or William Ford in "Jimmy Rose" are human beings and therefore limited; they learn their way around in the world as best they can, sharing their experiences and insights with the reader. Even Ishmael, who becomes absorbed into an omniscient voice that appears to project meaning, acknowledges the influence of his own "hypoes" on some of his best philosophizing, "The Whiteness of the Whale." Hence the burden of meaning rests, ultimately, on the reader; Melville's narrators are there to remind us that, in a complex world, truth never comes easily, if it comes at all.

The narrators of the five magazine works examined in this section reveal a variety of psychological and intellectual responses to experience, as Melville probes the internal workings of the self under various kinds of influence. Additionally, the way a narrator responds to experience controls the form of the narrative he relates. The sketcher in "The 'Gees" is only partially developed as a personality, but he is an ironic figure because his prejudice so obviously colors his characterization of the mulatto sailor. "The Fiddler" and "Cock-A-Doodle-Doo!" are more complex works of irony. In them Melville portrays narrators who are the victims of insecurity and egotism, and of some unfortunate reflexes as well. Finally, the

55

narrative protagonists in "The Lightning-Rod Man" and "The Apple-Tree Table" look for a set of spiritual values to help them live their lives, but, Melville suggests, the search for spiritual reality may yield only ambiguous answers.

"The 'Gees": The Narrator as Bigot

"The 'Gees" (*Harper's*, March 1856) is on the surface a humorous character sketch of a social "class," Portuguese-negro crossbreeds from Fogo. Descendants of convicts placed on the isle some centuries earlier, the 'Gees were gullible and ignorant, and they were occasionally recruited as sailors because they would work for little or no wages at all. The sketch has been given little critical attention, probably because it is such a slight production. Yet the fact that Melville would so carefully employ rhetorical irony in even a minor sketch suggests the degree of his commitment to irony in his magazine writings. Melville uses the persona of an engaging, worldly-wise sailor to characterize the 'Gee, and, as the opening paragraph would imply, there is no doubt something of Melville himself in the sketcher:

> In relating to my friends various passages of my sea-goings, I have at times had occasion to allude to that singular people the 'Gees, sometimes as casual acquaintances, sometimes as shipmates. Such allusions have been quite natural and easy. For instance, I have said *The two 'Gees*, just as another would say *The two Dutchmen*, or *The two Indians*. In fact, being myself so familiar with 'Gees, it seemed as if all the rest of the world must be. But not so. ("The 'Gees," p. 268)

Melville occasionally made fun of ignorant or physically unattractive sailors in his novels (Ropey in *Omoo*, for example), but in this piece he creates a persona that is ultimately distinct from himself as author. The rhetorical focus of the sketch is on the sketcher himself, who reveals his own insensitivity and inhumanity as he describes the inferiority and ignorance of the 'Gee.

Although he pretends to be an objective authority, from the start the seaman gives away his callousness and his strong bias against the 'Gee. "Of all men seamen have strong prejudices, particularly in the matter of race. They are bigots here. But when a creature of inferior race lives among them, there seems no bound to their disdain" ("The 'Gees," pp. 268–69). As far as the narrator is concerned, the 'Gee *is* a "creature of inferior race," and the rest of the sketch underscores his lack of compassion.

The sailor-narrator is a natural yarn-spinner, and he uses the standard tools of his trade—comic metaphor, exaggeration, and understatement. It is indicative of his own coarseness and insensitivity that his favorite satirical devices are animalistic metaphors and similes. Nature has fitted out the 'Gee in a "tough leather suit," he has "a serviceably hard heel" and can kick like a wild zebra, and to "know" a 'Gee one must study him as one would a horse: stand squarely before him and note "how he looks about the head, whether he carry it well; his ears, are they over-lengthy? How fares it in the withers? . . . How stands it in the region of the brisket?" ("The 'Gees," p. 272). And odor is another distinctive attribute of the 'Gee: "Like the negro, the 'Gee has a peculiar savour, but a different one—a sort of wild marine, gamey savour, as in the sea-bird called haglet" ("The 'Gees," p. 270).

Here the narrator becomes brutal in his similes, but at times his sense of humor seems healthier. For example, he explains that the 'Gees' "physicals and spirituals" are in "singular contrast." The 'Gee "has a great appetite, but little imagination; a large eyeball, but small insight. Biscuit he crunches, but sentiment he eschews" ("The 'Gees," p. 270). And after explaining that a "green" 'Gee is "of all green things the greenest," the knowledgeable seaman adds: "Besides, owing to the clumsiness of their feet . . . green 'Gees are wont, in no inconsiderable numbers, to fall overboard the first dark, squally night; insomuch that when unreasonable owners insist with a captain against his will upon a green 'Gee crew fore and aft, he will ship twice as many 'Gees as he would have shipped of Americans, so as to provide for all contingencies" ("The 'Gees," p. 271). Yet when the narrator attempts understatement or comic indirection, he invariably reveals anew his inhumane attitude toward the 'Gee: "But though any number of 'Gees are ever ready to be shipped, still it is by no means well to take them as they come. There is a choice even in 'Gees. . . . [T]here is no call to which the 'Gee will with more alacrity respond than the word 'Man!' Is there any hard work to be done, and the 'Gees stand round in sulks? 'Here, my men!' cries the mate. How they jump" ("The 'Gees," pp. 271–72, 274).

Toward the end of his sketch, Melville's ironically conceived narrator observes: "The innate disdain of regularly bred seamen towards 'Gees receives an added edge from this. The 'Gees undersell them, working for biscuit where the sailors demand dollars. Hence, any thing said by sailors to the prejudice of 'Gees should be received with caution" ("The 'Gees," p. 274). Parallel with Melville's technique in the other tales, the narrator consciously or unconsciously reveals preconceptions or biases which cast doubt upon the validity of his perceptions. As is the case with "Bartleby" or "Jimmy Rose," Melville's rhetoric in "The 'Gees" treats the common reader to an entertaining descriptive surface, which the more discriminating reader discovers "should be received with caution."

"The Fiddler" and "Cock-A-Doodle-Doo!": The Insecure Narrator

"The Fiddler" (*Harper's*, Sept. 1854) begins *in medias res*:

So my poem is damned, and immortal fame is not for me! I am nobody forever and ever. Intolerable fate!

Snatching my hat, I dashed down the criticism, and rushed out into Broadway.... (*SW*, p. 233)

Helmstone the poet starts his tale as does the narrator of "Cock-A-Doodle-Doo!": in an irritable mood and especially sensitive to things that antagonize him or threaten his ego. The initial signs are that neither protagonist will respond judiciously or rationally to experience. As a study of a rejected author, there is no doubt a good deal of Melville's own bitterness and exasperation with the literary marketplace in "The Fiddler." Similarly, "Cock-A-Doodle-Doo!" reveals Melville's impatience with a philosophy that, although it "sold" well, to him seemed naive: Emersonian Transcendentalism. Whatever personal history may be hidden away in the two stories, Melville's technique puts considerable ironic distance between each of his narrators' perspectives on reality and reality itself. "The Fiddler" is a minor piece, but its rhetorical method is carefully conceived. "Cock-A-Doodle-Doo!" may be Melville's most completely developed work of rhetorical irony prior to *The Confidence-Man*; once the story is under way, almost every narrative statement becomes suspect.

"The Fiddler" seems to have benefitted somewhat from Irving's "The Poor-Devil Author" (*Tales of a Traveller*). The egotistic narrator of this tale, who is a frustrated poet like Helmstone, is convinced that his lengthy masterpiece will take the literary world by storm. Unable to find a publisher, however, he goes bankrupt printing his own edition, which fails to attract a single critical notice. After a long series of disillusioning experiences, personal, artistic, and financial, the would-be author comes to his senses and settles for paid-by-the-line hackwork for the newspapers: "I gave up immortal fame to those who could live on air; took to writing for mere bread; and have ever since had a very tolerable life of it" (*TT*, p. 186).

Both the plot and theme of "The Poor-Devil Author" are echoed in "The Fiddler." Melville's petulant and self-centered poet, like Irving's, is denied "immortal fame" when his poem is rejected by the critics. However, the example of the fiddler, Hautboy,[1] a former child prodigy who is now happier without fame than with it, moves him to tear up all his manuscripts and buy himself a fiddle. Here Melville may be punning on the concluding motif in Irving's tale, the narrator's turn to hack writing. Eric Partridge notes that a mid-nineteenth-century meaning of the slang verb "fiddle" was "to make a living from small jobs done on the street."

Helmstone's moodiness and impulsiveness ironically reinforce the theme of patience and acceptance in "The Fiddler." When the protagonist rushes splenetically onto the street, he is "instantly soothed" by gazing on the face of his friend Standard's genial companion, the fiddler. His "intolerant pride" is, he admits, rebuked by Hautboy's "honest cheeriness" and by his blend of good sense and good humor. Now in a mood of calm reflection, he sees in Hautboy a man of "marvelous juvenility" who is "kind and honest," a person who accepted the world realistically. "[H]e did not theoretically espouse its bright side nor its dark side," and rejecting all solutions, "he but acknowledged facts" (*SW*, p. 235).

The narrator admits to Standard that he wishes that he himself were Hautboy. His friend replies, however, that there is only one Hautboy in the world; with the recollection of his own injured pride, the narrator's "dark mood" quickly returns. As in "Fragment No. 2," Melville's attention to the comic effects of human reflexes heightens the irony of the story. Suddenly "sneering with spleen," the narrator contradicts his previous conclusions about the fiddler's insights and retorts

1. William H. Gilman thinks that Melville's model for the fiddler was the brilliant young violinist and actor Joseph Burke (1815–1902), who had captivated English and Irish audiences before moving to America in 1830. Burke had come to Albany, New York, in 1834 and was living there at the same time that Melville and his family were; Melville may even have attended one of Burke's concerts (*Melville's Early Life and Redburn*, pp. 76, 316 n. 148).

that Hautboy's cheerfulness and good sense are undoubtedly owing to his being "[u]npossessed of genius." His spite and resentment grow rapidly in the following dialogue with Standard:

> [Standard suggests:] "You would not think him an extraordinary genius, then?"
> "Genius? What! such a short, fat fellow a genius! Genius, like Cassius, is lank. . . . Yes, Standard," cried I, increasing in spleen, "your cheery Hautboy, after all, is no pattern, no lesson for you and me. With average abilities; opinions clear, because circumscribed; passions docile, because they are feeble; a temper hilarious, because he was born to it. . . . Could ambition but prick him; had he but once heard applause, or endured contempt, a very different man would your Hautboy be. Acquiescent and calm from the cradle to the grave, he obviously slides through the crowd." (*SW*, pp. 236–37)

Contrary to what Helmstone thinks, Hautboy *is* a genius, had been first praised, then ignored, by the public, and could provide a lesson for us all.

The narrator remains unenlightened even when Standard drops hints about Hautboy's past. His irritated response to the announcement that Hautboy plays the fiddle is all the more ironic, because the narrator had himself delighted in one of his performances some years earlier. "Fiddle! thought I—he's a jiggumbob *fiddler*, then? No wonder genius declines to measure its pace to a fiddler's bow. My spleen was very strong on me now" (*SW*, p. 238). The story closes with Standard's revealing the fiddler's identity, but the culminating irony is that the narrator still does not comprehend the "pattern" or "lesson" that Hautboy provides. Instead of dedicating himself anew to literary endeavors more within his reach, no longer to concern himself with fame but instead with self-fulfillment and happiness, he tears up his manuscripts, buys a fiddle, and impractically rushes out "to take regular lessons" from Hautboy.[2]

The sources for "Cock-A-Doodle-Doo!" (*Harper's*, Dec. 1853) are both general and specific in nature. As he wrote his story, Melville was no doubt thinking of the traditional symbol of the vainglorious cock, found from Chaucer through Aesop, and in American folklore, as well.[3] Literary evidence also indicates that Melville's skepticism about the impetuous optimism of the Transcendentalists, and about the significance of their Eastern "crowing," is the real subject of "Cock-A-Doodle-Doo!" In fact, as we shall see, he may have had certain passages from Thoreau directly in mind as he wrote.[4]

2. R. K. Gupta claims that Melville's irony ambiguously undercuts the image of the fiddler, too. In his juvenility Hautboy is reminiscent of the ruddy Jimmy Rose, the superficial bachelors in "The Paradise of Bachelors," and youthful, naive Pierre. His philosophy is one of moderation, argues Gupta; rather than evincing real wisdom he settles for compromise and acquiescence, as does the sophistical Plinlimmon ("Hautboy and Plinlimmon: A Reinterpretation of Melville's 'The Fiddler,'" *American Literature*, 43 [Nov. 1971], 437–42). Yet Mr. Gupta does not mention that there is much in Hautboy that suggests Pip, who was carried down to the "everlasting, juvenile eternities" where he saw both the "joyous" and the "heartless" aspects of nature and experience (*Moby-Dick*, Ch. 93). Hautboy also echoes the major dynamic of Ishmael's mind: his wisdom had enabled him to entertain opposing ideas concurrently, and so, too, the fiddler espoused neither the "bright" nor the "dark" but saw them as aspects of existence.

3. Davy Crockett and Mike Fink often boasted of themselves as cocks, and a characteristic frontier fight challenge featured crowing and arm-flapping (Van Wyck Brooks, *The World of Washington Irving* [New York: Dutton, 1944], pp. 125–26). Cooper and Robert Montgomery Bird also depicted the "crowing" of rough-and-ready frontier characters (Kenneth S. Lynn, ed., *The Comic Tradition in America* [New York: Doubleday, 1958], pp. 258–59).

4. Egbert S. Oliver's arguments in "'Cock-A-Doodle-Doo!' and Transcendental Hocus-Pocus," *New England Quarterly*, 21 (June 1948), 204–16, are still convincing. He locates passages in "Monday," from *A Week on the Concord and Merrimack Rivers*, that suggest the central theme and symbol in Melville's tale. See Hershel Parker, "Mel-

Melville's narrator is yet another study in the effects of "hypoes" on personality. As the crowing cock on the doubloon was for Ahab, so the rooster in "Cock-A-Doodle-Doo!" is for the narrator a symbol of proud defiance; for both characters, however, the defiant stance is misguided, if not disastrous. Like the protagonist in "Fragment from a Writing-Desk," or like Redburn, the narrator begins his tale in an irritable and antagonistic mood. Moreover, he appears to have a fixation on discomfort and disease. The landscape imagery with which he opens his narrative reflects his splenetic temperament and his inability to view reality objectively. "It was a cool and misty, damp, disagreeable air. The country looked underdone, its raw juices squirting out all round. I buttoned out this squitchy air as well as I could . . . and spitefully thrusting my crab-stick into the oozy sod, bent my blue form to the steep ascent of the hill. This toiling posture brought my head pretty well earthward, as if I were in the act of butting it against the world. I marked the fact, but only grinned at it with a ghastly grin" (*SW*, p. 119). The narrator projects his mood onto the landscape, and thus it gives him back images of his own unhealthiness. "Along the base of one long range of heights ran a lagging, fever-and-agueish river, over which was a duplicate stream of dripping mist. . . . Afar . . . there rested a great flat canopy of haze, like a pall. . . . It was too heavy and lifeless to mount of itself; so there it lay, between the village and the sky, doubtless hiding many a man with the mumps, and many a queasy child" (*SW*, p. 120).

Working himself into an increasingly bilious frame of mind, the protagonist suddenly shifts his spitefulness, directing it against "thick-headed" engineers who cause steamboat wrecks but particularly against "that dunning fiend, my creditor" (*SW*, p. 121). For a major cause of the narrator's physical

----

ville's Satire of Emerson and Thoreau: An Evaluation of the Evidence," *American Transcendental Quarterly*, 7 (Summer 1970), 61–67, for an overview of Melville's literary response to the Transcendentalists.

discomfort and antagonism is his financial insecurity, appropriately symbolized in the person of the persistent dun:

[He] duns me even on Sunday, all the way to church and back, and comes and sits in the same pew with me, and pretending to be polite and hand me the prayer-book opened at the proper place, pokes his pesky bill under my nose in the very midst of my devotions, and so shoves himself between me and salvation; for how can one keep his temper on such occasions? (*SW*, p. 122)

Here Melville's rhetorical irony grows complex. It is, after all, not the dun that would prevent the narrator's salvation, but his own failure to meet his financial responsibilities.

In the passage following the one just quoted, the disease imagery is reiterated, only now it is more directly tied up in the narrator's mind with his own economic plight. Melville masterfully employs the comedy of involuntary gesture as the narrator leaps, by a process of free association, from his money problems, to sickness in others, to his own illness, to the price paid for charitable giving. "I can't pay this horrid man; and yet they say money was never so plentiful—a drug in the market; but blame me if I can get any of the drug, though there never was a sick man more in need of that particular sort of medicine. It's a lie; money ain't plentiful—feel of my pocket." The narrator promptly reaches into his pocket, and Melville records his reflex response: "Ha! here's a powder I was going to send to the sick baby in yonder hovel, where the Irish ditcher lives. That baby has the scarlet fever." This leads him to a morose and sardonic comment on the pointlessness of childhood suffering: "I suppose many of the poor little ones, after going through all this trouble, snap off short; and so they have had the measles, mumps, croup, scarlet fever, chicken pox, cholera morbus, summer-complaint, and all else, in vain!" (*SW*, p. 122).

He suddenly experiences a sympathetic rheumatic twinge

in his right shoulder. "I got it one night on the North River, when . . . I gave up my berth to a sick lady, and stayed on deck till morning in drizzling weather. There's the thanks one gets for charity! Twinge! Shoot away, ye rheumatics! Ye couldn't lay on worse if I were some villain who had murdered the lady instead of befriending her. Dyspepsia too," he suddenly remembers, "I am troubled with that" (*SW*, p. 122).

Melville's heavy use of imagery at the beginning of the story serves an important rhetorical function. As the narrator compulsively spills images of himself across the page, he but confesses his own instability. Then, abruptly, his personality seems to undergo a change. He hears "a triumphant thanksgiving of a cock-crow" and all at once finds himself "in rare spirits." Manic now, he begins chatting away about this extraordinary sound to a half-dozen calves grazing nearby, and the world suddenly sheds its diseased appearance and looks bright and promising. Melville's point, reinforced by his imagery, is that the narrator's vision of reality changes as radically as his moods change. Needing a way out of his economic troubles, he fixes on the cock's crowing as a call to battle. He literally throws the pesky dun out of doors, and slaps another mortgage on his house when the collector initiates a civil process against him. There was nothing to fear, however, for "Plain as cock could speak, it said, 'Hang the process, and hang the fellow who sent it! If you have not land or cash, go and thrash the fellow, and tell him you never mean to pay him. Be jolly!' " (*SW*, p. 135).

Determined to possess the fowl with the "clamorously-victorious" crow, the narrator spends several weeks roaming the countryside in quest of it. In time he learns that the poor Maryland wood-sawyer, Merrymusk, owns the proud Shanghai; Merrymusk refuses to sell the bird, however, because its crowing gives his ailing family "stuff against despair." It is at this point that the real object of Melville's satire, Transcendental optimism and self-reliance, becomes apparent. The narrator's belief in the cock's authority over his own irresponsible actions is now conjoined with Merrymusk's conviction that it can fortify the spirit and eliminate suffering. Merrymusk is "a glorious independent fellow," "a great philanthropist" who, through the medium of his crowing cock, gives "glorification away gratis." Thanks to the cock, the narrator, too, finds "glorification": "I felt as though I could meet Death, and invite him to dinner, and toast the Catacombs with him, in pure overflow of self-reliance and a sense of universal security" (*SW*, p. 128).

Yet the cock, finally, is an ineffectual barrier against his master's poverty and disease,[5] even as it proves a false source of inspiration for the narrator. Failing to attend to their wasting bodies, Merrymusk and his family die while relying only on their rooster's "triumphant" crowing to keep them from despair. Believing himself spiritually and psychologically rejuvenated, however, the narrator returns home still convinced that the defiant optimism by which the cock's owners lived—and died—would help him endure his own earthly trials. With almost maniacal exhilaration, he inscribes on the family's gravestone what he feels to be the perfect Transcendental epitaph:

> *O death, where is thy sting?*
> *O grave, where is thy victory?*

Never since then, he adds, "have I felt the doleful dumps, but under all circumstances crow late and early with a continual crow" (*SW*, p. 147). However, the reader must see the protagonist's experience in opposite terms: one cannot afford to be led blindly astray by a philosophy which views life neither steadily nor whole, nor should one take as a hero a narrator in psychological and moral disarray.

5. The cock's ineffectuality is underscored by means of two puns, one obvious and the other less so, on the fact that Merrymusk is from Maryland. First of all, the cock inspires the wood-sawyer to continue, however absurdly, to be "merry" in the face of despair. Secondly, one finds that Merrymusk has taken his home state's motto too literally: Maryland is traditionally known as the "cockade state."

"The Lightning-Rod Man" and "The Apple-Tree Table": The Ambiguous Pose

The ironic narrative strategies of "The Lightning-Rod Man" (*Putnam's*, Aug. 1854) and "The Apple-Tree Table" (*Putnam's*, May 1856) are especially telling indicators of the ways in which Melville's literary imagination shaped the complex world he saw. Philosophically, the stories echo the enigmatic questions that *Moby-Dick* had raised, for his two protagonists explore events which have theological as well as metaphysical overtones. In fact, the tales parallel to some extent the theme and conclusion of "The Town-Ho's Story," where the possibility of supernatural intervention in human affairs is raised, but the meaning of such intervention left unanswered. In a way the two stories form contrasting halves of an allegorical diptych on religious orthodoxy, and the two slightly manic narrators are psychologically kin. The first story portrays Calvinistic fatalism ironically, and in the second the narrator's uncertainty about Providence's role in human affairs also has ironic implications. In both works the Melvillean stance seems, finally, to be one of tentative compromise: the Unknown is, after all, unknowable, and both narrators—although one of them does not realize it—are denied the truth.

The two characters in the allegorical "Lightning-Rod Man" are humorously exaggerated mouthpieces for opposing theological positions. The story can be viewed as a double-edged satire, directed primarily against the cringing and pessimistic salesman who fears lest God's wrath strike him at any moment, but also against the overly devout narrator, who perhaps too readily accepts the Almighty's plan for him.

The sources for the tale contribute to its design and suggest ways in which Melville made use of contemporaneous materials for story ideas. Jay Leyda thinks that the tale may have developed around Melville's experience with a real lightning-rod salesman in Pittsfield, for in the fall of 1853 "the Berkshires were enduring an intense lightning-rod sales campaign, with advertisements and warnings on the subject in all the Berkshire papers."[6] Such a sales campaign may have proved the catalyst for the story, and it is apparent that Melville drew upon local history for some of the specific occurrences mentioned in the tale.[7] Leyda also learned that the Pittsfield Library had acquired a copy of Cotton Mather's *Magnalia Christi Americana* in 1853 and suggests that Melville could have read Chapter II, Book VI, "Ceraunius. Relating Remarkables Done by Thunder."[8] In this chapter Mather includes a sermon on the voice of God as manifested in thunder and lightning; elements in the sermon relevant to Melville's story are the assertions that the unrepentant sinful are afraid of the anger of God in the thunder but that true Christians should not be fearful.

Another source, thus far overlooked, deserves particular attention. Melville seems to have been a regular subscriber to *The Literary World*,[9] and of course he wrote several critical reviews for it from 1847 to 1850. Did he read the following anecdote in an 1849 book review of G. H. Lewes's *The Life of Maxmilien Robespierre*?

THE LIGHTNING ROD.

So early as 1783, I find Maxmilien called upon to defend an important case. The recent discoveries of Franklin had been adopted in France; and even in the province of Artois a . . . M. de Vissery de Boisville, had erected a lightning conductor on his property, much to the scandal of the worthy citizens. "What!" said they, "shall we rend the lightning from the hand of God? Shall man presume to intercept the wrath of the Deity[?] If God wills to destroy houses or farms, it is his will and pleasure—man's

6. *The Complete Stories of Herman Melville*, p. xxvi.
7. The narrator's allusions to an elm tree and an assembly-room that had been struck by lightning parallel events in contemporaneous Pittsfield history (*The Complete Stories of Herman Melville*, pp. 239–40, nn. 143.28, 143.29).
8. *The Complete Stories of Herman Melville*, pp. xxvi–xxvii.
9. Sealts, *Melville's Reading*, entry 327.

duty is to submit. These lightning conductors are but the impious thoughts of Deistical philosophy! Away with them!" Thus reasoned these obese and stupid citizens of Arras. Nay, more; they not only reasoned, they threatened the demolition of the conductor.[10]

In this anecdote, complete with its appropriate title, the attitudes of the townfolk are a model for those of the somewhat over-zealous narrator of the story. One thinks particularly of the narrator's tirade against the lightning-rod man near the end of the work: " '. . . you mere man who come here to put you and your pipestem between clay and sky, do you think that . . . you can thoroughly avert the supernal bolt? . . . Who has empowered you, you Tetzel, to peddle round your indulgences from divine ordinations? The hairs of our heads are numbered, and the days of our lives. In thunder as in sunshine, I stand at ease in the hands of my God. False negotiator, away!' " (*SW*, pp. 220–21).

When the sales campaign was on in Pittsfield Melville might have recalled the *Literary World* anecdote, for the similarities are striking: both accounts incorporate the ideas that man cannot presume to take the bolt from God's hands, that if lightning strikes it is God's will, that lightning rods are impious devices, and that man's duty is to stand at ease and submit to God's plan. Furthermore, in both works the lightning-rod believer is ordered to take his implements away; also, Melville's narrator effectively demolishes the salesman's rod at the close of the story, paralleling the citizens' threatened destruction of the proprietor's rod.

Sources in hand, Melville aims his satirical thrusts first of all at nineteenth-century Calvinistic Christianity, at those ministers who use warnings of doom and damnation as rhetorical leverage on unbelievers.[11] But he also levels an ironic blow

10. *Literary World*, 7 July 1849, p. 6.
11. See Hershel Parker, "Melville's Salesman Story," *Studies in Short Fiction*, 1 (Winter 1964), 154–58, for parallel commentary on Melville's religious satire in this story.

at the narrator's own beliefs. Melville does not imply that the narrator's confidence and his stance "at ease in the hands of my God" is the only tenable religious attitude. The Robespierre biographer had termed the inordinately pious citizens "obese and stupid," and Melville, though less overtly, faults his narrator for his stubbornness and offhanded fatalism. His enthusiasm for the "glorious," "fine," and "noble" storm is a little imprudent, after all. As a random electrical phenomenon, lightning probably has more scientific than theological import, and its powers have to be reckoned with. The narrator acknowledges that lightning had damaged a nearby church the previous week and killed a servant girl in Canada a year earlier; one of the bolts crashing outside his own house could just as arbitrarily destroy him.

Critics generally view "The Lightning-Rod Man" as religious allegory, but without exception they build their interpretations around the satanically portrayed character of the salesman, the "[f]alse negotiator" (*SW*, p. 221).[12] Melville's rhetorical irony cuts in two directions, however. He puns sexually and theologically when the salesman brags about the powers of his copper lightning-conductor, contending that the Canadian (Catholic) iron rods are faulty whereas his is "the only true rod." But is the narrator's "rod" any truer or more potent than either of these? Always the skeptic, Melville seems to choose the middle ground between total capitulation to fear, on the one hand, and blithely serene confidence in the efficacy of God's plan, on the other. Working through the humor and repartée of the story, Melville as implied author meditates on the dangers of total commitment to the dark or to the bright.

The humor of "The Apple-Tree Table, or, Original Spiritual Manifestations," was sufficient in itself to recommend the tale to the readers of the 1850's. Yet, as with "The Lightning-

12. See particularly Fogle, *Melville's Shorter Tales*, p. 55; Parker, "Melville's Salesman Story," p. 155; Ben D. Kimpel, "Melville's 'The Lightning-Rod Man,'" *American Literature*, 16 (March 1944), 30–31.

Rod Man," in "The Apple-Tree Table" the real issues of the story are hidden beneath its comic surface. The tale is a delightful piece of improvisation and narrative self-portraiture, characteristically Melvillean in its emphasis on comic gesture and reflex response. At the same time, the story raises the kinds of complex questions that disturbed Melville all of his life: what does nature symbolize, and what sway do the Devil and God have over events? Of more significance, perhaps, is the fact that the story subtly satirizes those who presume to have the answers to these questions.

In its digressiveness and anecdotal method the tale belongs in the mainstream of the Romantic essay. The narrator's antiquarian interest in old tables and old books is reminiscent of Irving's "London Antiques" in *The Sketch Book* or of Lamb's "Old China" in *Essays of Elia*, while the imagery of the garret where the table is found parallels motifs in Hawthorne's "The Old Manse."[13] Melville based the plot of his story on the familiar New England anecdote of an insect that ate its way out of an apple-tree table.[14] While Melville obviously had in mind the spirit-rapping fad of mid-century, it is possible, too, that he wrote his story as a satire on Thoreau's own adaptation of the apple-tree anecdote in *Walden*, where it serves as a parable of resurrection and immortality.[15]

The rhetorical strategy of the tale holds the key to its meaning. The subtitle of the story, "Original Spiritual Manifesta-

13. Edward Rosenberry observes that both Melville and Hawthorne describe in their sketches a gothic stairway entrance to a mysterious or romantic attic, allude to mouldy old books found within, and develop motifs of light and resurrection ("Melville and His *Mosses*," pp. 48–49).

14. Douglas Sackman first pointed out that Timothy Dwight's *Travels; in New-England and New-York* (1821–22) contains an account of the surprising emergence of a live insect from wood long dead, as does D. D. Field's *A History of Berkshire County* (1829). See "The Original of Melville's Apple-Tree Table," *American Literature*, 11 (Jan. 1940), 448–51.

15. See Frank Davidson, "Melville, Thoreau, and 'The Apple-Tree Table,'" *American Literature*, 25 (Jan. 1954), 479–88.

tions," implies that its real subject will be the spiritual significance of a physical object, but of course what is finally made "manifest" may be one thing to the narrator and something else to the reader. For in facing the mysteriously ticking table the protagonist not only must confront his own inner self but also his more public self, as head of his family. The narrative rhythm of the story is based primarily upon a series of reverses that occur in the narrator's inner and outer behavior towards the table. Behind these reverses—some of which the protagonist recognizes and some of which he does not—speaks Melville's ironic voice. The narrator is revealed as the victim, although to a large degree a sympathetic one, of his own unredeemable contradictoriness.

The major contradiction in the protagonist is that between his pretense towards practicality and objectivity, and his inherent superstitiousness and tendency to regard physical objects as symbols of occult mysteries. At the outset of his tale, for instance, the narrator proudly reveals that he had been able to acquire his old mansion at a bargain price, because rumors that the garret was haunted kept other buyers away. Although he personally dismissed these rumors as "absurd" and entertained "no dread of the reputed goblins" (SW, p. 409), he nevertheless had not once in his five years of residency entered the attic. "There was no special inducement," he quickly explains.

A curious old key found in the garden finally tempts him to try the locked garret door. He symbolically enters his own unconscious when he opens the door and in a labyrinth of cobwebs and mummified insects finds a dusty antique table with "a mouldy old book in the middle—Cotton Mather's *Magnalia*." The narrator's instinctive response to the table is an uneasy and superstitious one: "When I first saw the table, dingy and dusty . . . and set out with broken, be-crusted, old purple vials and flasks, and a ghostly, dismantled old quarto, it seemed just such a necromantic little old table as might have belonged to Friar Bacon. Two plain features it had, significant of conjurations and charms—the circle and tripod; the slab being round, supported by a twisted little pillar, which, about a foot from the bottom, sprawled out into three crooked legs, terminating in three cloven feet. A very Satanic-looking little old table, indeed" (*SW*, p. 409).

Yet the narrator's other self leads him to view the table, once carried downstairs and polished, as an eminently practical piece of domestic furniture; it would make a famous breakfast and tea-table, whist table, and reading-table. As the story progresses, the ironic confrontations between the narrator as he pretends to be and his more superstitious and insecure self increase. What he will later term as his inner contest between "panic and philosophy" begins, one night, when he is reading the *Magnalia* at his little table. Rather than being entertained by the book, as he had expected, he finds that he is disturbed by it. For he realizes that the terrifying accounts of witchcraft were written not by a Mrs. Radcliffe but by "practical, hard-working, earnest, upright" Reverend Mather. Moreover, many other "sound, worthy men," including that "matter-of-fact compiler of a dictionary," Samuel Johnson, had been believers in ghosts.

As the narrator, compulsively now, reads on in "doleful, ghostly, ghastly Cotton Mather" he inadvertently discloses that, beneath his confident exterior as man of the house and resolute handler of practical affairs, lurks a precariously balanced and ineffectual being. Like the narrator in "I and My Chimney," he is often self-conscious and irresolute in the face of his wife, who "was not wanting in firmness and energy" (*SW*, p. 414). She makes him feel guilty when he indulges in a tumbler or two of Saturday-night punch, and he had to be extraordinarily cautious on Sunday mornings as a consequence. Thus, when he suddenly hears a mysterious ticking in the parlor, "panic" immediately puts his insecure inner self to flight; after a cursory search round the room he quickly hurries off to bed. "Bless me, said I to myself, with a sudden revulsion, it must be very late; ain't that my wife calling me? Yes, yes; I must to bed" (*SW*, p. 417).

The next morning he tries unsuccessfully to convince his spouse that it was his excitement over the strange ticking, and not the punch, which caused him to stumble against a bedroom chair the night before; he also dresses with special care, to demonstrate his capability for grace under pressure. But it is apparent that Melville's hero has become psychologically rattled by his experiences when he starts making excuses for not using the table for breakfast or for his nightly reading; it really was too low, after all.

Recovering some of his self-confidence, and "resolved to regain the good opinion of my wife," on the next night the protagonist squares off before the table: "I drawled out, in as indifferent and dryly jocose a way as I could: 'Come, come, Tick my boy, fun enough for to-night' " (*SW*, p. 423). After all, sturdy Democritus had not permitted himself to be frightened by spurious ghosts. He is alone in the parlor when the ticking at last stops, and a beautiful insect crawls forth from the table. The next morning he quickly seizes the opportunity to claim heroic action for himself in "silencing" the ticking.

"Wife," said I, next morning, "you will not be troubled with any more ticking in our table. I have put a stop to all that."
"Indeed, husband," said she, with some incredulity.
"Yes, wife," returned I, perhaps a little vain-gloriously. "I have put a quietus upon that ticking. Depend upon it. The ticking will trouble you no more." (*SW*, p. 425)

The scornful wife has long since learned not to "depend" upon her husband's statements, and when the sound returns his magnificent victory goes for naught. The appearance of another insect prompts her to call in Professor Johnson, the local naturalist, for a rational explanation of the whole episode.

The narrative rhythm of the story underscores Melville's

philosophical theme. As the narrator explains, to the very end he "gently oscillated between Democritus and Cotton Mather." On the one hand, unlike his rationalistic wife or Professor Johnson, the narrator could never totally be a Democritus. To have adopted the Professor's strictly scientific explanation of the phenomenon of the insects' appearance would somehow have impaired their mystery and sparkling beauty and would also have marked the narrator's capitulation to his wife's camp. Melville, in fact, blatantly satirizes the scientist's calculation of the second bug's lifespan: the naturalist allows ninety years for the time the egg was in the living tree and eighty years for the age of the table, for a total of one hundred and *fifty* years. "Such, at least, was Professor Johnson's computation," says the narrator. On the other hand, the protagonist does not assert complete, unqualified belief in immortality, as symbolized for his daughter Julia by the "spiritual lesson" of the insect. Julia had ecstatically affirmed: " 'For if, after one hundred and fifty years' entombment, a mere insect comes forth at last into light, itself an effulgence, shall there be no glorified resurrection for the spirit of man? Spirits! spirits!' she exclaimed, with rapture, 'I still believe in spirits, only now I believe in them with delight, when before I but thought of them with terror.' " "The mysterious insect did not long enjoy its radiant life; it expired the next day," notes her more skeptical father (*SW*, p. 435).

Thoreau used the anecdote of the insect at the end of *Walden* to insist that "There is more day to dawn. The sun is but a morning star." [16] Melville, like his still edgy narrator, would choose the middle ground, and his story satirizes those who assume a knowledge beyond their ken. What Thoreau saw as a promise of spiritual transcendence, Melville accepted only as a possibility. Furthermore, the anxiety and indecision of Melville's narrator is laughable only up to a point. The appearance of the insects, after all, seemed as much a sign of the Devil's work as of God's miraculous intervention.

16. *Walden* (Columbus, Ohio: Charles E. Merrill, 1969), p. 357.

V

The Diptychs: The Rhetoric of Structure and Narration

Melville seems to have invented the diptych as a literary form in composing "The Two Temples" in the late winter or early spring of 1854. However, he had been exploring some of the rhetorical possibilities of contrasting sketches in earlier works. In Chapters 76 and 77 of *Mardi*, for example, Taji descriptively compares Donjalolo's House of the Morning to his House of the Afternoon. The contrasts between Chapters 74 and 75 of *Moby-Dick* are more complex, though, as Melville discusses both the physical and the philosophical differences between the sperm whale's head and the right whale's head. Melville was putting "The Encantadas" into final form just before he began "The Two Temples," and perhaps the differences between the "humanity" of the Chola widow, in Sketch Eighth, and the hermit Oberlus, in Sketch Ninth, suggested further literary applications of paired sketches.

However Melville discovered the form, his diptychs proved to be successful experiments in short narrative. At first glance, the contrasting but related "pictures" in "The Two Temples," "Poor Man's Pudding and Rich Man's Crumbs," and "The Paradise of Bachelors and the Tartarus of Maids" appear to be little more than social essays, comparing British and American institutions and attitudes. Yet the structure and narrative method of the diptychs give them a rhetorical power that belies their seemingly facile artistry. In each pair of sketches, as critics have suggested, the whole is in effect greater than the sum of its parts. The motifs and patterns in the second half of each diptych evoke the first half and implicitly comment upon it, even as a rereading of the first part evokes the second. At the same time, Melville's subtle use of ironic first-person narration increases the satiric force of his sketches. Melville's narrators see themselves as observers and social critics of sorts, but in different ways each becomes a victim of the institution that he holds up for criticism.

"The Two Temples"

Melville submitted "The Two Temples" to *Putnam's New Monthly Magazine* in the spring of 1854, only to have it rejected by the editor because he thought it might offend some readers' sensibilities. Melville wrote his sketch in part to satirize the ostentatiousness of churchgoing at a certain anonymous "temple" in New York, but the *Putnam's* editor recognized the object of Melville's criticism: Grace Church. The church was first opened in 1846 and was known to be exclusive;[1] Melville apparently saw it as a fruit ripe for the picking. In addition, Melville's contemporaries may have offered literary models for the sketch. Both Irving's "The Country Church" (*The Sketch Book*) and Hawthorne's "Sights from a Steeple" (*Twice-Told Tales*) are sketches of the occupations, social status, and personal attributes of individuals who pass before the narrator's gaze as he sits at a convenient vantage point. Irving's satirical comments on a well-fed parish official and on the hypocritical opulence and show of several parishioners in an English church are especially suggestive of "Temple First."

Melville's carefully modulated point of view in the diptych reinforces its themes. As was the case with the protagonist in "Cock-A-Doodle-Doo!" the financial insecurity of Melville's narrator-observer has led him to experience a degree of psychological insecurity as well. He needs to feel a sense of com-

1. Leyda, *The Complete Stories of Herman Melville*, p. 462 note.

munity, but in "Temple First" a heavy-faced beadle denies his "humble petition" for entry into the fashionable New York church. This would not have happened, the protagonist defensively explains to himself, had he had his new topcoat with him and been able to tickle the man's palm with a banknote. His pride rebuked, he lurks about the glistening marble edifice, wishing he were seated alongside the wealthy aristocrats within. He at last manages to gain entry into the tower through a side door, but the image of the church warden and his embarrassment about his own shabby appearance and possible misconduct increase his sense of insecurity: "The beadle-faced man . . . was just in the act of driving three ragged little boys into the middle of the street; and how could I help trembling at the apprehension of his discovering a rebellious caitiff like me peering down on him from the tower? For, in stealing up here, I had set at naught his high authority. He whom he thought effectually ejected had burglariously returned" (*SW*, p. 151).

Focusing on the narrator's reflex actions is, again, a major technique in Melville's humor. The narrator jumps when the organ begins to play, thinking that the warden has sounded the alarm; when the service is over, and he finds the door locked from without, he nearly panics. Nervously reascending the tower, then descending, only to ascend again, he repeatedly asks himself, "What is to be done?" Knocking on the door, he worries self-consciously, would expose him to the beadle: "and if he sees me, he will recognize me, and perhaps roundly rate me—poor, humble worshipper—before the entire public" (*SW*, pp. 154–55). Finally, he decides to announce himself "magnanimously" by ringing the bell, to "forestall an inglorious detection." His last thought, before being pulled out of the doorway by the warden and taken to the judge, is predictably melodramatic: "Nothing will serve me now but the reckless confidence of innocence reduced to desperation" (*SW*, p. 156).

Melville suits narrative method to theme. The protagonist is an insecure figure with a shaky self-image who needs the communion and fellowship that should have been available in the church; it is ironic that he is coldly turned away—and even more ironic that the magistrate fines him for having illegally been in church.

"Temple Second" begins a month or so later. After his "inglorious expulsion," the narrator had packed up his bags and his "damaged character" for Philadelphia, where by chance he had obtained a position as a traveling companion and physician for two ladies. Once again he experiences rejection, however: they cavalierly dismiss him in London, and he suddenly finds himself without a cent. After almost drowning in the surging throngs of people on the main streets, he escapes up a side lane and sees before him a solemn, cathedral-like structure. It proves to be a theater, and the celebrated Charles Macready is performing that night. Convinced that an evening in the theater could "revive" his jaded spirits, he even thinks of pawning his overcoat for admittance; unexpectedly, however, a working-man generously gives the narrator his ticket. Realizing that he has received charity for the first time in his life, the narrator is at first ashamed, but he quickly sees how foolish he would be, alone and penniless in London, to deny the warm gesture of one man to another. He soon takes his seat in the upper gallery.

Melville's point is that the narrator has a truer spiritual experience, and finds more human compassion, in the second "temple." First of all, Macready's performance as Cardinal Richelieu is sincere and therefore honestly inspiring, whereas in the New York church the narrator had the feeling that he was viewing a "sly enchanter's show" below him. The priest's motions were studied, his tone carefully "melodious," and his sermon to his wealthy parishioners ironically misdirected—"Ye are the salt of the earth" had been his text. Moreover, the protagonist had found authentic fellowship with the English workers in the gallery. Symbolic of sacrifice and charitable ministering to human need, a ragged boy, despite his own poverty, had even given the narrator a free mug of porter.

Wellingborough Redburn's youthful observations on churchgoing may foreshadow Melville's thesis in "The Two Temples." "It is a most Christian thing, and a matter most sweet to dwell upon and simmer over in solitude, that any poor sinner may go to church wherever he pleases. . . . I say, this consideration of the hospitality and democracy in churches, is a most Christian and charming thought" (*Redburn*, p. 203). With experience comes disillusionment, and the narrator of "The Two Temples" finds, paradoxically, that an American church may place the aristocrat before the common man. The English, however, seem capable of making an almost religious form of communion possible even outside the institutional walls of the church.

"Poor Man's Pudding and Rich Man's Crumbs"

"Poor Man's Pudding and Rich Man's Crumbs" (*Harper's*, June 1854) also features contrasting American and English sketches, but here Melville intends the reader to see parallels as well in the social and philanthropical philosophies represented in the two countries. Thematically, "Bartleby," "The Two Temples," "Poor Man's Pudding and Rich Man's Crumbs," and "Jimmy Rose" are related: all confront the problem of the proper charitable stance towards those who are deprived, if not forsaken, economically and socially. As F. O. Matthiessen contends, the "economic factor in tragedy" appeared at every stage of Melville's writing. Redburn and Ishmael went to sea in part because they were out of money, and the later novel *The Confidence-Man* is "built around characters who are made fools or knaves by money."[2] Yet Melville was especially concerned with the subject of charity in the middle 1850's. His general point in the stories listed above is

2. *American Renaissance* (New York: Oxford Univ. Press, 1941), pp. 400–01.

that mankind is either ignorantly complacent or naively optimistic about the plight of the impoverished.[3]

"Poor Man's Pudding" tacitly criticizes the pseudophilanthropist who views the poor sentimentally and romantically, and rationalizes his own basic uncharitableness. As the sketch opens, the celebrated but appropriately named poet "Blandmour" explains that the poor have nothing to be concerned about because they can extract so much comfort and sustenance from Nature's gifts. Rain-water, particularly, serves as "Poor Man's Manure" and "Poor Man's Eye-water," and helps to make "Poor Man's Egg," "Poor Man's Plaster," and "Poor Man's Pudding." When the narrator is given an unpalatable meal at the damp, decaying home of the poverty-ridden Coulters, he sees that Blandmour's assumptions and theories about the poor are inadequate; however, in failing to confront Blandmour with his discoveries he himself ironically adopts the poet's complacent stance.

Melville may have written this half of his diptych in reaction to the kind of sentimental fiction so prevalent in his day. A popular novel in the 1840's was Catharine Maria Sedgwick's *The Poor Rich Man and The Rich Poor Man* (first published in 1837), the naiveté and insensitivity of which could have helped inspire his sketch, while the title served his ironic purposes.[4] A contemporaneous review of the novel adequately

3. In several essays Marvin Fisher has examined Melville's treatment in his short fiction of social injustice and of the moral and spiritual failure of society; in this connection Fisher compares Melville's tales with Joyce's *Dubliners* and Anderson's *Winesburg, Ohio*. See "Focus on Melville's 'The Two Temples': The Denigration of the American Dream," in *American Dreams, American Nightmares*, ed. David Madden (Carbondale, Ill.: Southern Illinois Univ. Press, 1970), pp. 76–86; "Melville's 'Tartarus': The Deflowering of New England," *American Quarterly*, 23 (Spring 1971), 79–100; " 'Poor Man's Pudding': Melville's Meditation on Grace," *American Transcendental Quarterly*, 13 (Winter 1972), 32–36.

4. Catharine Sedgwick was raised in Lenox and Berkshire County, and she and her family were known to the Melvilles (see Jeanne C. Howes, "Melville's Sensitive Years," in *Melville and Hawthorne in*

sums up its thesis: "A full appreciation by the poorer and humbler classes . . . of their proper station in the social economy, their responsibilities and advantages, is what is needed. In them a spirit of contentment, not of ambition, should be fostered. The Creator has given to such, sources of enjoyment peculiar to their condition, which others, in their different spheres, know not of."[5] Even the reviewer himself falls into the sentimentalist trap.

Melville could not have helped scoffing at the superficiality and lack of understanding evinced by the writers of works like this one by Miss Sedgwick. As Rosenberry has suggested, the poet Blandmour is a naive optimist of the same type satirized by Melville in *Pierre*.[6] The following heavily ironic authorial observation from Melville's novel would apply to Miss Sedgwick, as well as to Blandmour:

> If the grown man of taste, possess not only some eye to detect the picturesque in the natural landscape, so also, has he as keen a perception of what may not unfitly be here styled the *povertiresque* in the social landscape. To such an one, not more picturesquely conspicuous is the dismantled thatch in a painted cottage of Gainsborough, than the time-tangled and want-thinned locks of a beggar, *povertiresquely* diversifying those snug little cabinet-pictures of the world, which, exquisitely varnished and

the Berkshires, ed. Howard P. Vincent [Kent, Ohio: Kent State Univ. Press, 1968], p. 30). Melville had talked with Henry Dwight Sedgwick, Jr., during the famous picnic climb up Monument Mountain in August, 1850, and Luther Mansfield believes that Catharine's sister-in-law may also have attended the festivities ("Melville and Hawthorne in the Berkshires," in *Melville and Hawthorne in the Berkshires*, p. 11). Melville no doubt knew Catharine's popular *Hope Leslie* (1827), in which, as Mansfield reminds us, a Pequod Indian maiden plays a significant role.

5. Robert Walsh, reviewer, *American Quarterly Review*, 21 (March 1837), 20.

6. *Melville and the Comic Spirit* (Cambridge, Mass.: Harvard Univ. Press, 1955), p. 162.

framed, are hung up in the drawing-room minds of humane men of taste, and amiable philosophers of either the "Compensation," or "Optimist" school [Emerson and others]. They deny that any misery is in the world. . . . Go to! [they say] God . . . hath bounteously blessed the world with a summer carpet of green. Begone, Heraclitus! The lamentations of the rain are but to make us our rainbows! (*Pierre*, pp. 276–77; italics Melville's)

The water imagery of "Poor Man's Pudding" underscores through ironic counterpoint the limitations of Blandmour's "drawing-room mind"—especially his contention that Nature's "gift" of water serves the poor so completely. The narrator quietly brushes cold, damp flakes from his clothes as he listens to Blandmour speak enthusiastically of "this soft March snow" as a beneficial "Poor Man's Eye-water" (*SW*, p. 168), and when the narrator yields to his friend's urging and goes to Coulter's hut for a bowl of "Poor Man's Pudding," the pattern of imagery becomes thematically insistent. He arrives on a wet Monday noon and finds Dame Coulter finishing her wash, meanwhile standing on a "half-rotten, soaked board to protect her feet, as well as might be, from the penetrating damp of the bare ground." It is no surprise that the poor woman "look[s] pale and chill"; the child she is carrying adds to her paleness, moreover, and its life can only be one of sickness and deprivation.

Water as a force for decay and deterioration, rather than as a heavenly bounty, permeates the house. The fire logs are "old and damp" and make a "sad hissing, and vain spluttering"; the building itself is old, "and constitutionally damp. The window-sills had beads of exuded dampness upon them. The shriveled sashes shook in their frames, and the green panes of glass were clouded with the long thaw" (*SW*, p. 171). When Poor Man Coulter arrives for a hasty lunch of mouldy pork, "[t]he moisture ooze[s] from his patched boots," and as he leaves to chop wood in "the soak and the mire" his wife speaks of her cheerless existence: "I am left so lonesome now; day after day, all the day long, dear William is gone; and all the damp day long grief drizzles and drizzles down on my soul" (*SW*, p. 175). Through the imagery of his sketch Melville suggests that human experience often ironically contradicts the assumptions of "the well-housed, well-warmed, and well-fed" (*SW*, p. 177).

The second half of the diptych, "Rich Man's Crumbs," grew directly out of one of Melville's own experiences in London in 1849. He had attended the Lord Mayor's Show on November 9 (a "most bloated pomp" he called it) and the next day had been guided by a city official to the famous charity traditionally held after the Lord Mayor's Day festivities: "... I pushed my way through cellars & anti-lanes into the rear of Guildhall, with a crowd of beggars who were going to receive the broken meats & pies from yesterday's grand banquet (Lord Mayor's Day).—Within the hall, the scene was comical. Under the flaming banners & devices, were old broken tables set out with heaps of [left-over] fowls, hams, &c. (A good thing might be made of this.)."[7]

In making a "good thing" out of this experience Melville portrayed the primitive violence to which deprivation and famine had reduced the London beggars. In contrast to the Coulters' passive acceptance of poverty, the thought of sweet-meats and other delicacies left over for the poor turned the English beggars into a "mob of cannibals," a bestial pack of "ferocious creatures" mad with hunger. Melville's sardonic catalog of the paltry scraps of meat and pastry tossed to the poor is a prologue for the inevitable conclusion of the event, when the unsatisfied mob, in a spontaneous explosion of violence, wrecks the banquet hall to protest the insincerity as well as the insufficiency of the "noble charity." Like Blandmour, the city functionary who takes the narrator to the hall is unresponsive to real human need, and he brags about the "mag-

7. Eleanor Melville Metcalf, ed., *Journal of a Visit to London and the Continent* (Cambridge, Mass.: Harvard Univ. Press, 1948), p. 26.

nanimous" charity so unselfishly given by the Lord Mayor. Melville's design in this particular diptych was to contrast by understatement "the practical misery and infamy of [American] poverty" in the first half with the "all too thoroughly accepted" British poverty in the second part.[8] We are left with the impression that, on both sides of the Atlantic, a combination of politics, "national character," and a misguided sense of benevolence has furthered rather than eased the plight of the poor.[9] Melville, on the one hand, disparages American politics and society for fostering a false sense of democratic pride and "equality" among both the rich and the poor; the American paupers' hesitancy to accept charity and their awareness of "the smarting distinction between their ideal of universal equality and their grindstone experience" (*SW*, p. 176) are the primary reasons for their unrelieved wretchedness. British society, on the other hand, blithely accepts poverty as an institution worthy of both praise and show.

Melville's first-person narrative technique helps to broaden the social implications of his sketch. As the narrator guides us across the two social landscapes, Melville forces us, rhetorically, to draw conclusions about the narrator—and about the real import of what he witnesses—that he himself is unwilling to face. He had "half choked" on the bitter and mouldy Poor Man's Pudding and had left Dame Coulter's house "laden down" with a sense of the "deleterious quality" of its atmosphere. Yet that evening, as he sat on Blandmour's "comfortable sofa, before a blazing fire, with one of his two ruddy little

8. Fogle, *Melville's Shorter Tales*, p. 41.
9. A few years later, in *The Confidence-Man*, Ch. 1, Melville gave ironic treatment to the charitable virtues enumerated in I Corinthians 13. One virtue in particular, "Charity never faileth," notes Edwin Honig, "suggests the benevolent effects of philanthropic virtue, but it must also be regarded as a self-righteous scruple which opposes the testimony of experience and thereby cruelly fails, as the novel shows, because it does not recognize the real, particular needs of individuals" (*Dark Conceit: The Making of Allegory* [Evanston, Ill.: Northwestern Univ. Press, 1959], p. 198 n. 9).

children" on his knee, he sums up his experience with an observation that, in effect, denies that either he or Blandmour have any responsibility toward the poor: "[Blandmour,] you are not what may rightly be called a rich man; you have a fair competence; no more. Is it not so? Well, then, I do not include *you*, when I say, that if ever a Rich Man speaks prosperously to me of a Poor Man, I shall set it down as—I won't mention the word" (*SW*, p. 177). At the conclusion of the second sketch, the narrator's disavowal is repeated. He had almost been trampled by the outraged mob of beggars at the Lord Mayor's Charity earlier in the day, and that night as he lay "bruised and battered" on his bed he sighed: "Now, Heaven in its kind mercy save me from the noble charities of London . . . and Heaven save me equally from the 'Poor Man's Pudding' and the 'Rich Man's Crumbs' " (*SW*, p. 184). The question directed to the reader comes as a type of social and moral challenge: who, then, is going to save the poor?

"The Paradise of Bachelors and the Tartarus of Maids"

Of the three diptychs, "The Paradise of Bachelors and the Tartarus of Maids" (*Harper's*, April 1855) has received the greatest scholarly attention. On the surface, the first half of the sketch is a characteristically Melvillean celebration of bachelorhood, and one finds in it echoes of the bachelor suppers and "smoking club" gatherings in *Typee*, *Mardi*, and *White-Jacket*. Yet critics have also found "The Paradise of Bachelors" to be of surprising psycho-sexual complexity, as "anatomical" in its own way as the more overtly punning "Tartarus of Maids." The two parts, however, have never been adequately examined in the context of their sources, and in terms of Melville's literary method. As with the unpublished Agatha material and "Benito Cereno," here we have an opportunity to view, in cross-section, Melville's adaptation of his sources to his aesthetic and intellectual vision.

To compose the first half of his sketch Melville began with recollections of his own 1849 sojourn in the Temple Bar *environs* of London (the home of the original order of Templars Crusaders), added descriptive motifs and background information from a current guidebook account of the area, and drew on an essay by Lamb and some motifs in Irving to help give his sketch form. Entries for 1849 in his *Journal of a Visit to London and the Continent* indicate that he paid a series of visits to Temple Bar. In November he had made a general walking tour through the Temple courts and gardens and visited Temple Church. There, "Saw the 10 Crusaders—those who had been to the Holy Land, with their legs crossed. Heads of the [knights] damned fine" (*A Visit to London*, p. 36). A month later Melville was back in the area following up some dinner invitations, and his journal entries for December 20, 21, and 23 provide the core for the banquet scene in "Paradise of Bachelors":

> Last night dined in Elm Court, Temple, and had a glorious time till noon of night. A set of fine fellows indeed. It recalled poor Lamb's "Old Benchers". . . . Up in the 5th story we dined. The Paradise of Batchelors [sic]. Home & to bed at 12.

> Last night dined at the Erechtheum Club St. James's with Mr. Cooke . . . nine sat down—fine dinner. . . . An exceedingly agreeable company.

> [again at the Erechtheum Club] . . . a party of eight. . . . We had a glorious time & parted at about midnight. (*A Visit to London*, pp. 77, 79, 80–81)

When Melville began to work his notebook material into sketch form for *Harper's*, he incorporated the nine who had sat down at the Erechtheum Club: nine genial bachelors are present at the dinner described in the sketch (Melville's choice of this number may have been reinforced by the fact that his sources told him there were nine knights in the original order of Templars). In addition his notebook comments for November gave him material for a description of the knights' tombs, although Melville turned to Charles Knight's guidebook, *Cyclopaedia of London* (1851), for specific descriptive motifs as well as background information appropriate to his needs. Knight's comment that in Temple Bar, centuries ago, "the haughty soldier's armed heel rang on the pavement, and the red cross was displayed on each resident's mantle"[10] is echoed in various passages in "The Paradise of Bachelors," and Knight's observations on the "troubled lives and chequered fortunes" of the early Templars and on the failings of some of the modern Templar-lawyers may have helped focus Melville's satire in the first sketch.

Another important influence on Melville's sketch was Lamb's "The Old Benchers of the Inner Temple," in *Essays of Elia*. Both works relate humorous and sentimental anecdotes about Benchers past and present, and, in fact, Melville was thinking of Lamb's reference to the bachelors' haunts as a "Paradise"[11] when he used the phrase "Paradise of Batchelors" in his *Journal*.

Once again, however, it is Irving who looms largest in the background of Melville's sketch. While generally paralleling Irving's emphasis on bachelor "sociality" and experience, Melville also seems to have drawn upon imagistic and thematic patterns in "London Antiques" (*The Sketch Book*) and "An Old Soldier" (*Bracebridge Hall*). In Irving, Melville discovered both a way of introducing his narrator's experiences at Temple Bar, and a rhetorical strategy for undercutting ironically the image of carefree bachelorhood.

The similar descriptions of Temple Bar in "London Antiques" and the first half of Melville's diptych have been briefly noted by William Hedges;[12] my point in mentioning them again here is to indicate that Melville was not at all reluctant to appropriate entire passages from his sources when

10. *Cyclopaedia of London* (London: Charles Knight, 1851), p. 446.
11. *Essays of Elia* (London: Macmillan and Co., 1899), p. 119.
12. *Washington Irving*, pp. 159–60.

he found them useful, descriptively or thematically. In fact, the whole first page of Melville's sketch is a paraphrase of Irving's picture of Temple Bar. Both writers describe the area as a secluded and refreshing oasis away from the crowds and hectic commercial world of downtown London, and Irving's imagery of quiet retreat suits Melville's theme of the London bachelors' withdrawal from active life.

Melville follows motifs in Irving's "An Old Soldier" in developing the satirical patterns in his story. Irving's sketch portrays a corpulent old general with a double chin whose polished deportment and considerable experience as a campaigner at watering-places, rather than battlefields, would make him a perfect companion-at-table in Melville's bachelor hall. A "blade of the old school" with powdered head, a rose in his buttonhole, and sweeping bows for the ladies, the bachelor general is also a gallant. During interludes in his dinner-table gossip Irving's bachelor frequently talks about "the service" and likes to hum the old song:

> Why, soldiers, why
> Should we be melancholy, boys?
> Why, soldiers, why,
> Whose business 't is to die!
>
> (*BH*, p. 58)

"I cannot discover, however," Crayon notes ironically, "that the general has ever run any great risk of dying, excepting from an apoplexy or an indigestion." Echoing Irving's sardonic attitude, in "Paradise of Bachelors" Melville's narrator laments the modern Knights-Templars' reduction "from carving out immortal fame in glorious battling for the Holy Land, to the carving of roast-mutton at a dinner-board" and observes that these "degenerate" Templars apparently "think it sweeter far to fall in banquet than in war."

Like one of Melville's Templar-lawyers, secure from the world's troubles in his cozy retreat near Temple Bar and well-provisioned for any siege, Irving's old general had made sure to spend his time in the garrison rather than on the field of Mars. His retirement is only an extension of what had been his life: " 'They talk of public distress,' said the general this day to me, at dinner, as he smacked a glass of rich burgundy, and cast his eyes about the ample board; 'they talk of public distress, but where do we find it, sir? I see none. I see no reason any one has to complain. Take my word for it, sir, this talk about public distress is all humbug!' " (*BH*, p. 59). Melville expands Irving's image of the ineffectual and unconcerned bachelor-general to include the whole order of modern-day Knights Templars: "The thing called pain, the bugbear styled trouble—those two legends seemed preposterous to their bachelor imaginations. How could men of liberal sense . . . and convivial understandings—how could they suffer themselves to be imposed upon by such monkish fables? Pain! Trouble! . . . No such thing.—Pass the sherry, sir" (*SW*, 193–94).

Melville's imagination and moral sensibilities imposed formal coherence upon his sources, and "The Paradise of Bachelors" becomes a subtle commentary on physical and spiritual impotence.[13] Rhetorically, the burden of analysis falls upon the reader; he must distinguish carefully between the moral issues of the story and the attractiveness of life at Temple Bar. Melville's vision in this sketch thus parallels that in "Jimmy Rose." The first-person narrator is an ironically developed figure

13. Four studies have contributed to my analysis of the diptych. Alvin Sandberg, in "Erotic Patterns in *The Paradise of Bachelors and The Tartarus of Maids*," *Literature and Psychology*, 18, No. 1 (1968), 2–8, discusses the apparent impotency of the narrator and the masturbatory quality of some of the incidents in the first sketch; Beryl Rowland similarly characterizes the narrator as an impotent figure who shows signs of a castration complex in the second sketch ("Melville's Bachelors and Maids: Interpretation Through Symbol and Metaphor," *American Literature*, 41 [Nov. 1969], 389–405). M. L. Pops, in *The Melville Archetype* (Kent, Ohio: Kent State Univ. Press, 1970), speaks of the phallic symbolism of the horn of snuff (p. 149), while W. R. Thompson emphasizes the political, economic, and spiritual vacuity of the Temple Bar lawyers' lives (" 'The Paradise of Bachelors and the Tartarus of Maids': A Reinterpretation," *American Quarterly*, 9 [Spring 1957], 34–45).

who is overcome by the artificialities and social elegance of the bachelors' life-style. He prefers not to acknowledge what his finer senses tell him: that the modern-day Knights Templars, as had Rose, lead unfulfilled and insignificant lives. Although the narrator acknowledges at the beginning of "The Paradise of Bachelors" that the modern Templar is at best a paltry representative of the old order, he soon loses his critical objectivity. He rationalizes that the knight's fall "has made him all the finer fellow," for he is no longer proud, gruff, and "hard" but instead "genial," "mellow," and hospitable. The modern Templar is a Jimmy Rose in his salad days: "His wit and wine are both of sparkling brands" (*SW*, p. 187). The narrator's glorification of his Temple Bar acquaintances soon reaches a sentimentalized crescendo: "If the having warm hearts and warmer welcomes, full minds and fuller cellars, and giving good advice and glorious dinners, spiced with rare divertisements of fun and fancy, merit immortal mention, set down, ye muses, the names of R. F. C.[14] and his imperial brother" (*SW*, p. 188).

The narrator lightly recounts his evening's festivities in the bachelor dining room and so thoroughly enjoys himself that he says no more to denigrate his "band of brothers." With a spontaneous "burst of admiring candor" he exclaims to his smiling host, "Sir, this is the very Paradise of Bachelors!" At the end of the sketch, however, Melville hints, once again, at the impotence of bachelor hall. After dinner the lawyers regale themselves with an immense phallic horn of snuff and later in the evening exit "two by two," some men going home to read the *Decameron* before retiring. For personal fulfillment, the bachelor-knights are capable only of turning inward upon themselves, homosexually or autoerotically, instead of outwardly to battles of spiritual conviction.

"The Tartarus of Maids" serves contrapuntally to underscore the human inadequacies conveyed in "The Paradise of Bachelors," and, once again, Melville's own experiences formed

14. Robert Francis Cooke, one of Melville's friends at Temple Bar.

the basic framework of his sketch, while his knowledge of the Berkshires helped him round out his piece imagistically. Leyda thinks that the piece grew out of Melville's winter paper-buying trips in the early 1850's to Carson's "Old Red Mill" in Dalton, which lies five or six miles from Pittsfield, and the descriptions of the workers and milling equipment in "The Tartarus of Maids" are no doubt based on what he saw on these expeditions.[15] As several critics have noticed, the first few pages of the work describe through an elaborate system of puns a trip down the front of the female anatomy, followed by an account of the sex act. If the reader of Melville's day saw only a description of a sleigh trip through the White Mountains, it was because the actual names for certain parts of the local topography almost exactly suited Melville's ironic and humorous purposes.

For instance, the Bellows-pipe, leading to the narrow pass called the Notch, is identified by the narrator as the "Mad Maid's Bellows-pipe," conjoined with the "Black Notch"; or, at the end of the anatomical journey, Melville relabels the Hopper, into which flows a tributary of the Green River, as the womb-like "Devil's Dungeon" complete with a turbidly menstrual "Blood River." Melville saw his punning as a way of toying with his readers' sensibilities. Furthermore, the narrator's symbolic sexual experience on his way to the paper mill (where, Melville puns, as a "seedsman" he intends to buy envelopes for seed-containers) is an ironic contrast to the physical celibacy as well as the spiritual withdrawal of the bachelors. His symbolical experience also contrasts with the inhuman "mating" of the pale maids to the machines they are forced to serve.

As Melville's sexual allegory grows more obvious it becomes less playful. The machines seemingly have taken over the sacred reproductive processes themselves from the factory girls; for example, it requires only nine minutes for the white, germinal pulp to go from the "abdominal heat" of the vats

15. *Complete Stories*, p. xxviii.

to the waiting arms of an attendant—a former nurse—as finished paper. In serving as slaves to the wants of the iron animals the maids even become their own executioners, for in the "consumptive pallors" of the rag-shredding room they are slowly murdered by inhaling the rag-dust from the cutting scythes which they must constantly sharpen.[16]

Taken in its entirety, Melville's diptych yields important insights into the author's attitudes towards mid-nineteenth-century civilization. W. R. Thompson contends that the two sketches are more than wry satires on "New World industrialism" and "Old World leisure"; they are an explicit expression of Melville's concern about the "inertia" and spiritual emptiness of both European and American society.[17] Melville also seems to be specifically warning us that if man permits machines to take over his biological responsibilities, at least symbolically if not actually, may not mechanism someday force him to abdicate moral and social control, too? The proud manager of the factory, Old Bach, is appropriately named, for he is insensitive to the physical and mental strain which his female workers must endure. Oblivious, too, is his assistant Cupid, who serves as pimp for the girls by arranging and supervising their perverted "marriage" to the machines.

Basic to the meaning of the second story, and a direct function of Melville's method, is the final response of the narrator to what he has witnessed. Despite his skepticism about the

16. Could Melville have had in mind Hawthorne's "The Procession of Life" (*Mosses from an Old Manse*, 1846) when he described the rag room? In Hawthorne's sketch the servitude of the seamstresses to their masters also leads to a consumptive death: "But what is this cloud of pale-cheeked, slender girls, who disturb the ear with the multiplicity of their short, dry coughs? They are seamstresses, who have plied the daily and nightly needle in the service of master tailors and close-fisted contractors, until it is now almost time for each to hem the borders of her own shroud. Consumption points their place in the procession" (*Mosses from an Old Manse* [Boston: Houghton-Mifflin, 1882], p. 238).

17. " 'The Paradise of Bachelors and the Tartarus of Maids': A Reinterpretation," passim.

working conditions in the factory, he nevertheless allows himself to become yet another victim of dehumanizing mechanism; in withholding criticism, he is similar to the narrator in "Poor Man's Pudding and Rich Man's Crumbs." He is awed by "the metallic necessity" which governs the machinery, and, although he fears that somehow mankind itself is being flattened and rolled in the grim inevitability of the engines, not once does he consider cancelling his order with the mill. The machine's "autocratic cunning" and its "unbudging fatality" hold him spellbound. As Beryl Rowland suggests, in both halves of the diptych the narrator-guide is primarily a voyeur who has insufficient strength of character to change or, for that matter, even to criticize openly what he sees.[18]

18. "Melville's Bachelors and Maids," passim.

VI

Experiments in Omniscience

"The Bell-Tower" (*Putnam's*, Aug. 1855) and "Benito Cereno" (*Putnam's*, Oct., Nov., Dec. 1855) are anomalies among Melville's magazine works. Temporarily abandoning the Crayonesque self-portraying narrator, Melville chooses instead the third-person, limited-omniscient voice. Melville's technique in his two tales is essentially Poe's classic method in the so-called detective stories. Like "Murders in the Rue Morgue," the two stories are designed as elaborate riddles in detection, and their solution reveals that inhuman forces of annihilation have been at work; as in Poe, the last several pages of "The Bell-Tower" and "Benito Cereno" provide explanations of the preceding mysterious events and at least partially clear up ambiguities.

Hawthorne's works also influenced Melville's two stories. In "The Bell-Tower," as I shall demonstrate, he draws several motifs directly from Hawthorne in writing his own allegory on creativity and the role of the artist. In a more general way, "Benito Cereno" suggests the reorientation of Melville's vision following his introduction to Hawthorne in 1850. This story probes the "power of blackness" in human nature and develops the archetypal theme Hawthorne so frequently treated: the innocent's initiation into evil.

Melville's two stories were successful as magazine pieces, but as art they differ considerably. In "The Bell-Tower" Melville's commitment to an allegorical formula imposes certain structural restraints on his narrative, denying him sufficient latitude for improvisation in theme and character. "Benito Cereno," however, is one of Melville's most rhetorically effective tales. Through limited omniscient narration Melville hints at the real condition of things aboard the *San Dominick*, while portraying Delano's confused quest for the truth. The imagery, furthermore, adds to the rhetorical power of his story. It intensifies the atmosphere of the tale, and, in a more subtle way, it helps to give external form to the horror and violence that have ravaged Don Benito's soul.

"The Bell-Tower"

Melville was familiar with most of the great allegories, *Everyman*, *The Faerie Queene*, *Pilgrim's Progress*, *The Divine Comedy*, and *Paradise Lost*, and had designed *Mardi* as an allegorical romance. And yet, suggests Randall Stewart, it was Melville's encounter with Hawthorne's *Mosses* in 1850 and the ensuing relationship between the two writers that seem to have prompted him to try further experiments with allegory.[1] In his review of the *Mosses*, Melville responded to the "blackness" and the "intellectual complexity" of Hawthorne's works, and he especially admired Goodman Brown's "allegorical pursuit of his Puritan wife." Although *Moby-Dick* was surely influenced by Hawthorne's allegorical vision of blackness, "The Bell-Tower" is Melville's most overt attempt at allegory in the Hawthornean manner. In fact, there is substantial literary evidence to indicate that "The Bell-Tower" is an ironic variation of "The Artist of the Beautiful," another story that Melville had praised in his review.[2] Additionally, Mel-

1. "Melville and Hawthorne," *South Atlantic Quarterly*, 51 (July 1952), 442.
2. Portions of this discussion appeared in my essay, "The Minor Fiction of Hawthorne and Melville" (cited above). Richard Fogle first noted the parallels between the two stories (*Melville's Shorter Tales*, p. 68 n. 3), and I investigated the possibility of direct influence in my dissertation, "Literary Influences and Technique in Melville's Short Fiction: 1853–1856" (1969). In his dissertation, "The Shock of Recognition: A Psycho-Literary Study of Hawthorne's Influence on Melville's Short Fiction" (1970), Wallace Christy finds parallels as well between Melville's story and "The Birthmark" and "Rappaccini's

ville drew motifs from *The Faerie Queene* as he developed the allegorical implications of his tale.

The ingenious artisans in "The Artist of the Beautiful" and "The Bell-Tower" sense their own superiority to society and isolate themselves from it, while seeking to endow a mechanical device with life-like attributes. Both succeed in their attempts, but of course Hawthorne's artisan learns to accept his butterfly as merely a man-made symbol of God-given beauty, whereas Bannadonna's overweening pride in his almost impious creation ultimately brings about his death. Time is a central theme in both works also. Owen Warland is a recalcitrant watchsmith who tries to transcend the pressures of the practical world and its demand for properly-adjusted timepieces; Bannadonna, the reverse image of Owen, constructs an elaborate clock mechanism to serve time and to bring fame to himself and his state, only to be destroyed by time's servant in the end. The motif of the "dance of the hours" in both stories suggests the transient nature of the two artisans' creations. Owen occasionally decorated clock faces with the twelve mirthful or melancholy hours, and in the course of time his spiritualized butterfly is destroyed by the material grasp of Danforth's son. Bannadonna is killed by his own mechanism while he is trying to alter the strange look on one of the twelve

Daughter." See also Irving Malin, "The Compulsive Design," in *American Dreams, American Nightmares,* pp. 67–69; Ray B. Browne, *Melville's Drive to Humanism* (Lafayette, Ind.: Purdue Univ. Studies, 1971), p. 253; Hershel Parker, ed., *Shorter Works of Hawthorne and Melville,* pp. 4–5.

Gerard M. Sweeney, in "Melville's Hawthornian Bell-Tower: A Fairy-Tale Source," *American Literature,* 45 (May 1973), 279–85, compares Melville's story to "The Minotaur," in *Tanglewood Tales* (1853). "Talus, the Man of Brass," in Hawthorne's Theseus tale is similar in many points to Melville's Talus, although the name originally came from Spenser (see text, below).

Critics have cited non-Hawthornean sources for Melville's tale, too: in Spenser, in Mary Shelley's *Frankenstein,* and in Cellini's *Life.* See Sweeney (mentioned above) and Robert E. Morsberger, "Melville's 'The Bell-Tower' and Benvenuto Cellini," *American Literature,* 44 (Nov. 1972), 459–62.

hours engraved on his newly cast bell. The mechanical creature is destroyed, and a year later the bell-tower itself falls in ruin.

The influence of *The Faerie Queene* can also be documented. In naming Bannadonna's mechanical man "Talus" Melville makes a suggestive allusion to a figure in Book V, and to a central theme in Spenser's allegory as a whole: the quest for virtue. Astraea gave her groom Artegall, a personification of Justice, a faithful servant in the form of an iron man:

> His name was *Talus*, made of yron mould,
> Immoveable, resistlesse, without end;
> Who in his hand an yron flale did hould,
> With which he thresht out falsehood, and did
> truth unfould.[3]

Spenser's Talus was a half-human creature with remarkable powers: he could defeat entire armies of brigands with his iron flail, and, most important, could recognize (and quickly punish) false and evil men. Melville's Talus, too, was "resistlesse," and by killing Bannadonna with his iron hands he seems instinctively to have unfolded truth and "thresht out falsehood." In a moment of pride and "esthetic passion" (*SW*, p. 358) Bannadonna had killed a worker, striking a piece of the man's flesh into the molten bell-metal. Bannadonna paid the price of justice with his own life, and his flawed bell plummeted to earth soon afterwards.

Although well supplied with motifs from his sources, Melville composed his story a little too self-consciously. The tale's studied archaisms and somewhat perfunctory plot are the result of his attempt to write a Renaissance allegory *as* an allegory, rather than to create meaning more organically around incident and character. In the *Putnam's* version Melville begins his story with three portentous epigraphs, which suggest that

3. *The Poetical Works of Edmund Spenser* (London: Oxford Univ. Press, 1909), II, Book V, p. 166.

the themes of ambition and the overthrow of a master will be illustrated allegorically:

> Like negroes, these powers own man sullenly; mindful of their higher master; while serving, plot revenge.
>
> The world is apoplectic with high-living of ambition; and apoplexy has its fall.
>
> Seeking to conquer a larger liberty, man but extends the empire of necessity. (*SW*, p. 355)

In the 1856 *Piazza Tales* edition of the story Melville omits the epigraphs. He probably saw them as revealing too much of the plot, while making the story's meaning too matter-of-fact. Yet he did not revise his heavily moralized conclusion for *The Piazza Tales*, and it is equally matter-of-fact: "So the blind slave obeyed its blinder lord; but, in obedience, slew him. So the creator was killed by the creature. So the bell was too heavy for the tower. So the bell's main weakness was where man's blood had flawed it. And so pride went before the fall" (*SW*, p. 372).

Apparently, Melville felt that the allegorical form obliged him to clear up most of the ambiguities of his tale. Although the magistrates had wondered whether the domino were alive, and a majority of citizens were convinced that a "supernatural agency" had intervened to destroy the impious artisan, Melville's recapitulation at the end of the tale is factual and, for all practical purposes, scientifically complete. It is obvious that Bannadonna's death had come, predictably and appropriately, at the hands of his own bell-striker.

However, Melville's use of contrasting organic and inorganic imagery in "The Bell-Tower" is more aesthetically satisfying; in fact, Melville's imagery broadens the philosophical scope of his tale in ways that the narrative proper could not. The triumph of the organic over the inorganic suggests the inevitability of death in the natural cycle of things and reinforces ironically the impermanence and ineffectuality of man's most ambitious creations.

Proud Bannadonna had tried not only to rival nature but to "rule her." With an "unheard-of degree of daring," he saw himself as a new Prometheus serving mankind by "supplying nothing less than a supplement to the Six Days' Work; stocking the earth with a new serf, more useful than the ox, swifter than the dolphin, stronger than the lion, more cunning than the ape, for industry an ant, more fiery than serpents, and yet, in patience, another ass" (*SW*, p. 368). Bannadonna's mechanical servant, in short, was to combine "all excellences of all God-made creatures, which served man." Yet the power compressed in the mechanism's coiled springs destroyed its haughty creator instead of serving him, and Bannadonna's "original production . . . terrible to behold" soon rusted, futilely, on the bottom of the sea. The cycle of justice had completed itself with the artist's death, and so too the natural cycle is completed at the story's close. A year after Bannadonna's death an earthquake toppled his proud tower, the symbol of his life; overthrown on the plain, the stones and bell-works were soon covered with lichens and moss, nature's shroud. Thus Bannadonna's tower had at last found its permanence, in decay.

"Benito Cereno"

Chapter 18 of Captain Amasa Delano's *Narrative of Voyages and Travels*[4] reported an incident that, to Melville's literary

4. *A Narrative of Voyages and Travels, in the northern and southern hemispheres: comprising three voyages round the world, together with a voyage of survey and discovery in the Pacific Ocean and Oriental Islands*, 2nd ed. (Boston: E. G. House, 1817), pp. 318–53. Harold H. Scudder, in "Melville's *Benito Cereno* and Captain Delano's *Voyages*," *PMLA*, 43 (June 1928), 502–32, documented Melville's use of his source. Melville's story, Chapter 18 of Delano's narrative, pertinent critical essays, and a list of textual variants have been collected in John P. Runden, ed., *Melville's "Benito Cereno"* (Boston: D. C. Heath, 1966).

imagination, must have seemed fraught with a "suggestiveness" equal to that in the Agatha material. Delano had for several hours given personal assistance to a Spanish slave trader that was short of water and supplies; the whole time he was on board, however, he was unaware that the slaves had rebelled and, even before his eyes, were holding the Spanish captain and crew in brutal subjection. Furthermore, Melville's source provided him with a compelling cast of characters. Like Agatha and Robertson, Captain Delano, Benito Cereno, and his black attendant were prototypes from real life; given careful psychological and emotional development, they would readily serve the tale's larger metaphysical themes.

In recreating his source materials as art, Melville worked a variation on his characteristic rhetorical mode, first-person ironic narration. He sought a method for hinting at Delano's incomplete view of reality, yet at the same time he wanted to preserve the immediacy and familiarity of the first-person technique, which had proven itself artistically seaworthy in his previous writings. What he settled on was a limited-omniscient narrator, one privileged to enter Delano's mind alone, but also permitted to draw partially aside the masks that conceal the identities of Babo and Cereno. Melville conceived his tale as an interior psychological portrait of the American captain, counterpointed by an alternately increasing and decreasing atmospheric pressure of suspense as Delano wavers between uneasiness and restored confidence. Also, Delano's responses to the enigmatical and disconcerting figure of Cereno, like the lawyer's to his scrivener, vary in both pitch and intensity: from objective deliberation (the ship's misfortune has resulted in an unusual state of affairs on board), to irritation and petulance (Cereno's impoliteness and reserve are an insult to a fellow sea-officer), to worldly-wise indulgence (Cereno is merely an incompetent), to near-panic (Cereno is a plotting pirate only waiting for an opportune moment to call his armed men out of the hold), to self-reproach (the poor fellow has suffered greatly, after all; the idea of a plot is absurd).

The tale thus moves with a studied uncertainty towards its climax, as the narrator explores Delano's subjective responses to Cereno and to the scenes which shape and reshape themselves before his eyes. As Berthoff explains, the story is a kind of riddle that the reader, no less than Delano, must solve: "The states of mind Captain Delano passes through are not, after all, essentially different from the ordinary ways by which we move, more or less blindly, through our works and days. So the story can fairly be seen as composing a paradigm of the secret ambiguity of appearances—an old theme with Melville—and, more particularly, a paradigm of the inward life of ordinary consciousness, with all its mysterious shifts, penetrations, and side-slippings." Melville's emphasis on Delano's thought processes and states of mind, rather than on dramatic action or event, is his way of stating, indirectly, that this is a world in which "ambiguity of appearances is the baffling norm."[5]

Another Melvillean "bachelor," good-natured Delano is naively confident about the world, and about his own God-given potentialities as a leader of men of will and benefactor of those weaker than himself. Out of his naiveté arises both a sense of superiority and a conviction that one is treated as he treats others. But Delano is also perceptually obtuse: he is unwilling and unable to allow his intuitive glimpses of the truth to overturn his preconceived notions about reality and human nature. The historical Delano had seen the central irony in his own experiences with the slaves, and Melville would follow it up in his story: "[The slaves] all looked up to me as a benefactor; and as I was deceived in them, I did them every possible kindness. Had it been otherwise there is no doubt I should have fallen a victim to their power. It was to my great advantage, that, on this occasion, the temperament of my mind was unusually pleasant. The apparent sufferings of those about me had softened my feelings into sympathy, or, doubtless my

5. *The Example of Melville*, p. 153. John Seelye has noted that there are some one hundred and fifteen "conjectural expressions" in "Benito Cereno" (*Melville: The Ironic Diagram*, p. 105).

interference with some of their transactions would have cost me my life."[6] Both Delano and Melville were struck by the fortune that can sometimes attend incomplete vision. Too thorough an understanding of reality can precipitate dangerous reflex actions; in Delano's obtuseness lies his salvation, and, for the moment at least, Don Benito's as well.

In retrospect, Captain Delano seems an almost transparently ironic figure and we are surprised at our own failure to see "around" him earlier than we do. The American captain is "blunt-thinking," "a man of such native simplicity as to be incapable of satire or irony," and "a person of singularly undistrustful good nature, not liable, except on extraordinary and repeated incentives, and hardly then, to indulge in personal alarms, any way involving the imputation of malign evil in man" (*SW*, p. 256). Melville also plays more subtle variations on his rhetorical method, giving Delano ironic thoughts or having him make ironic statements to poor Cereno. At one point, for instance, Delano observes to himself that the Spanish captain's authority over the Negro slaves seems to have been impaired. Delano's conclusion is in fact correct, but his reasoning is faulty: he assumes that lack of water and long-continued suffering brought on the misrule aboard ship. Or, when the psychologically and physically debilitated Don Benito collapses into the arms of ever-present Babo, Delano exclaims, " 'Faithful fellow! . . . Don Benito, I envy you such a friend; slave I cannot call him!' " Again, the good-natured captain speaks more than he knows. Delano's musings on the tableau before him further compound the irony: "As master and man stood before him, the black upholding the white, Captain Delano could not but bethink him of the beauty of that relationship which could present such a spectacle of fidelity on the one hand and confidence on the other" (*SW*, p. 270).

Melville's narrative method carefully prepares the reader for the culminating irony of the story. In spite of what they have experienced together, Delano understands as little about

6. Runden, *Melville's "Benito Cereno,"* p. 80.

Cereno's spiritual and psychological state at the end as he did at the beginning of their relationship. To the last Delano remains an innocent, for even after learning of Babo's atrocities he fails to see why the broken-spirited Don Benito cannot forget the past. In the final conversation between the two captains, Delano's comments on the natural landscape not inappropriately echo the lawyer's when he visited Bartleby in prison and tried to lift his spirits by pointing out the sky and the grass:

> "But the past is passed; why moralize upon it? Forget it. See, yon bright sun has forgotten it all, and the blue sea, and the blue sky; these have turned over new leaves."
>
> "Because they have no memory," he dejectedly replied; "because they are not human."
>
> "But these mild trades that now fan your cheek, do they not come with a human-like healing to you? Warm friends, steadfast friends are the trades."
>
> "With their steadfastness they but waft me to my tomb, Señor," was the foreboding response.
>
> "You are saved," cried Captain Delano, more and more astonished and pained; "you are saved: what has cast such a shadow upon you?"
>
> "The negro." (*SW*, pp. 351–52)

And Melville terminates the dialogue fittingly: "There was no more conversation that day." Don Benito Cereno died a short time after this meeting, psychologically annihilated, and Melville suggests that the "steadfastness" of Delano's incomprehension also helped to waft the pale Spaniard to his tomb.

The imagery of "Benito Cereno" counterpoints Delano's interior monologue: Melville's images establish and reinforce mood, while they also symbolize the disintegrated psyche of the Spanish captain. In its basic form the tale is a meditation upon the texture of reality. For Delano reality is a flux of ambiguous images, but for Benito the images of reality are static, their meaning horribly apparent. As Berthoff explains,

Melville conveys the images of "Benito Cereno" in a succession of tableaux, or descriptive set-pieces.[7] The images that compose these tableaux fall into two patterns. Motifs of ambiguity and unreality dominate Delano's field of vision and probably the reader's as well, his first time through the tale; at the same time, images of physical deterioration, brutality, and death inject into the tale's ambiguousness a disquieting sense of pending violence and destruction. It is these images of decay and physical violence that come to represent the tormented consciousness of Don Benito.

The most celebrated of Melville's tableaux opens the narrative and suggests the forthcoming ambiguities and veiled tensions between blackness and whiteness. On the morning that marked Delano's encounter with the Spanish slave ship, "everything" was mute, calm, and gray: "The sea, though undulated into long roods of swells, seemed fixed, and was sleeked at the surface like waved lead that has cooled and set in the smelter's mold. The sky seemed a gray surtout. Flights of troubled gray fowl, kith and kin with flights of troubled gray vapors among which they were mixed, skimmed low and fitfully over the waters . . ." (*SW*, p. 255). Melville closes his description with the pithy aside, "Shadows present, foreshadowing deeper shadows to come."

Having set the stage generally with a mood of ambiguity and uncertainty, Melville reinforces his theme through more specific scenes. For instance, Delano's glimpse of the noisy throng of blacks and whites as he steps over the *San Dominick*'s bulwarks has "the effect of enchantment": "The ship seems unreal; these strange costumes, gestures, and faces, but a shadowy tableau just emerged from the deep . . ." (*SW*, p. 260). Two elements from this tableau, the four black oakum-pickers and the six hatchet-polishers, are pictured again at later points in the story. The artificial disposition of these figures, and the awkward playacting of Babo and Cereno, make Delano vaguely apprehensive; he senses that he is viewing a masquer-

7. *The Example of Melville*, p. 69.

ade, arranged for some deceitful purpose. Delano is right, of course, but he is a man reluctant to yield his "reason" to his intuition.

Motifs of decay, brutality, and death—the second major pattern of imagery—augment the threatening quality of the atmosphere, but they also help to generate additional levels of meaning in the story. The Negroes aboard the *San Dominick* are compared to the Black Friars, the Dominicans who conducted the Inquisition; mastering both the mind and the body of Cereno, they even extract "false confessions" from him, for Delano's benefit. Cereno's vessel, furthermore, is likened to the monastery to which Charles V of Spain retired, and it serves as a fitting symbol of the faded glory and strength of the Spanish empire. Melville's story thus becomes a kind of allegory on the confrontation of primitive Africa, civilized Europe, and naive America, and on the destruction and spiritual loss attendant upon political and religious upheaval.

More specifically, however, these images represent the horribly debilitating effects of Cereno's experience. The *San Dominick* itself is the most dramatic symbol of her captain's suffering: "Battered and mouldy, the castellated forecastle seemed some ancient turret, long ago taken by assault, and then left to decay." In an allusion to the decline of both the Spanish empire and Cereno's authority, Melville adds: "the principal relic of faded grandeur was the ample oval of the shield-like stern-piece, intricately carved with the arms of Castile and Leon, medallioned about by groups of mythological or symbolical devices; uppermost and central of which was a dark satyr in a mask, holding his foot on the prostrate neck of a writhing figure, likewise masked" (*SW*, pp. 258–59). The stern-piece is an appropriately ambiguous symbol of the story's various "masked" characters, both conquered and conquering. Cereno and Babo wear "masks," although Babo is the real "dark satyr," Cereno's malevolent conqueror. Of course, Delano is the figure who, in a very literal sense, comes to hold

Babo underfoot and "prostrate," when the Negro tries to kill Cereno aboard the American's longboat.

The tableau of the cuddy, like the ship itself, symbolizes the psychological torture that Cereno has undergone. In this chamber, where the Spanish captain was kept prisoner, is a "clawfooted old table" underneath which lie "a dented cutlass or two" and a "hacked harpoon." Nearby are "two long, sharpribbed settees . . . uncomfortable to look at as inquisitors' racks," and "a large, misshapen arm-chair, which, furnished with a rude barber's crotch at the back, working with a screw, seemed some grotesque engine of torment" (*SW*, p. 305). While making Cereno's suffering more "visible," these motifs also reinforce in the story a mood of threatening violence and psychic horror.

Motifs of death and incarceration serve two aesthetic and rhetorical purposes. They provide, in retrospect, a continual reminder of the slaughter that has taken place aboard the *San Dominick*, even as they foreshadow Don Benito's incarceration in the monastery and, finally, his death. Appropriately, then, Melville describes the sea-grass draping the vessel as "mourning weeds" and notes the "hearse-like roll of the hull" (*SW*, p. 259). Built into the cabin wall, furthermore, are "small, round dead-lights—all closed like the coppered eyes of the coffined," and the cabin door is "calked fast like a sarcophagus lid."

In the tableau that concludes the tale, Melville turns again to a motif in his source. Among the documents pertaining to the trial is the official court sentence, pronouncing that the heads of the leaders of the murderous rebellion be "fixed on a pole" in the town square and their bodies burned. In Melville's story black Babo, symbol of depravity and hatred, receives the same judgment. The Black had cast his shadow over Don Benito, and it drove the Spanish captain to his grave. Yet even though the Negro, too, found his own "voiceless end," his blackness lived on as a force for deception and evil. Babo's head, "that hive of subtlety, fixed on a pole in the Plaza, met, unabashed, the gaze of the whites" and looked toward the monastery where Cereno soon died. In his final ironic gesture Melville implies that Babo, even after death, remains the master of man's spirit and fate. His dead head looks out over the world and his inhumanity somehow still arranges the events of the universe.

VII

Form as Vision: The Organicism of "The Encantadas"

In "The Encantadas" (*Putnam's*, March, April, May 1854), Melville returns after a three-year's absence to the familiar ground of the travel narrative, and it is not surprising that the guide-figure in the sketches is philosophically reminiscent of the Ishmael of *Moby-Dick* days. Although Melville was by no means contemplating another work of such epic proportions, we do know that previous to the publication of the ten sketches he had been planning a book on tortoise-hunting; apparently he changed his mind and adapted to magazine form whatever material he had already written.[1] "The Encantadas," like *Moby-Dick*, went through a complex "trying-out" as Melville carefully synthesized his own experiences and his source materials.

While serving on the *Acushnet*, in November 1841, Melville visited the archipelago of the Galápagos (Spanish for "tortoises") or Encantadas Isles, and internal evidence in the sketches indicates that he did some exploring on at least one of the islands. It appears, also, that Melville reached the archipelago again in late 1842 or early 1843, on the *Charles and Henry*, leaving him with a goodly supply of recollections, or at least impressions, with which to round out the information gleaned from his sources. For there was a surprising amount of literature available on the Galápagos, and he seems to have

1. See Howard, *Herman Melville*, pp. 209, 211.

109

familiarized himself with much of it.[2] At the end of "Sketch Fifth" he lists the primary sources from which he often paraphrased or drew direct quotations: *Captain Cowley's Voyage Round the Globe* (vol. IV of William Dampier, *A Collection of Voyages, in Four Volumes* [1729]), James Colnett, *A Voyage to the South Atlantic* (1798), and David Porter, *Journal of a Cruise Made to the Pacific Ocean* (1815). Other probable sources, which Melville did not cite, are John Coulter, *Adventures in the Pacific* (1845), and Charles Darwin, *Journal of Researches . . . during the Voyage of H.M.S. Beagle* (1839).[3]

Melville's goal was to bring the sketches out of his researches and memory into structural and thematic coherence, and there is some disagreement about his success in doing so. Ronald Mason and Newton Arvin admire the "fierce generation of mood" and the "extraordinary harmony of image and feeling" in the sketches, but each finds them too loosely constructed to warrant the term high art.[4] Richard Fogle, however, is convinced that the sketches achieve unity in the theme of the Fall and in Melville's repeated use of visual sensations to make the wasteland archipelago "known" to the reader.[5] As a more recent analysis suggests, Melville's vision in "The Encantadas" is essentially a dualistic one.[6] Melville's rhetorical technique is to develop throughout the sketches a series of opposing tensions, meanwhile hinting that a metaphysical and moral order

2. The most complete study of Melville's sources is Russell Thomas's "Melville's Use of Some Sources in *The Encantadas*," *American Literature*, 3 (Jan. 1932), 432–56.

3. A full bibliography of writings on the Galápagos can be found in Victor Wolfgang Von Hagen's *Ecuador and the Galapagos Islands* (Norman, Okla.: Univ. of Oklahoma Press, 1940), pp. 265–79.

4. Mason, *The Spirit Above the Dust* (London: John Lehmann, 1951), p. 188. Arvin, *Herman Melville* (New York: Viking Press, 1964), p. 241.

5. *Melville's Shorter Tales*, pp. 93, 114.

6. One of the best discussions in print of the technique of "The Encantadas" is Margaret Yarina's essay, "The Dualistic Vision of Herman Melville's 'The Encantadas,'" *Journal of Narrative Technique*, 3 (May 1973), 141–48. In some ways my analysis parallels Professor Yarina's.

will be found among the isles once these tensions are resolved. It is, finally, the reader's job to resolve them, thereby discovering for himself the aesthetic and philosophical unity of "The Encantadas."

The first two sketches in the series, "The Isles at Large" and "Two Sides to a Tortoise," introduce Melville's dialectic by stating or implying a series of contrasts between the islands' "darker" and "brighter" aspects. The archipelago seems an uninhabitable wasteland, and yet it has a considerable population of living things, from lizards and birds to men; the archipelago is a fallen world where "the chief sound of life . . . is a hiss," and yet, as a later sketch would show, the islands would also prove to be a place of heroic patience and spiritual triumph for Hunilla, the Chola widow; the islands are volcanic piles, fused and immovable, and yet they are the "wandring isles," capricious and "unmappable." Melville plays variations on this set of opposing tensions in contrasting the unchangeable nature of the Galápagos ("[cut] by the Equator, they know not autumn, and they know not spring"), with the strange transformations and enchantments that the islands have worked on their inhabitants and visitors, tortoises and men alike.

The major tension in the sketches, finally, is that between the stark reality of the Galápagos and their baffling unreality and supernatural quality. What the senses tell the observer about the islands is insufficient, we find, for the "archipelago of aridities" leaves its most meaningful impressions at a deeper level: in the psyche. Melville's narrator-observer closes Sketch First with the somewhat embarrassed admission that the Encantadas had affected him mentally, for they had, absurd to say, made him a believer in enchantments. Occasionally, sitting among blasted pines in some deep-wooded gorge of the Adirondacks, and remembering, "as in a dream," his rovings "in the baked heart of the charmed isles," the narrator would recall images of dusky shells and of vitreous island rocks grooved by the slow draggings of the tortoise. At these times, he admits, "I can hardly resist the feeling that . . . I have indeed slept upon evilly enchanted ground" (*SW*, p. 54). The narrator sometimes wonders, nervously, if he is not also the "occasional victim of optical delusion [sic] concerning the Galapagos."

> For, often in scenes of social merriment, and especially at revels held by candle-light in old-fashioned mansions, so that shadows are thrown into the further recesses of an angular and spacious room, making them put on a look of haunted undergrowth of lonely woods, I have drawn the attention of my comrades by my fixed gaze and sudden change of air, as I have seemed to see, slowly emerging from those imagined solitudes, and heavily crawling along the floor, the ghost of a gigantic tortoise, with 'Memento [Mori]' burning in live letters upon his back. (*SW*, p. 54)

The narrator has seen no mere "optical delusion"; his vision is a primal one, apocalyptic in nature, and it arises out of his own unconscious response to the mysterious landscape of the Encantadas.

"The Isles at Large" and "Two Sides to a Tortoise" also establish the image patterns that will give descriptive texture and atmosphere to the series of sketches. These images are an essential part of Melville's dialectic, for when they are fused in the reader's mind they help to reveal the artistic and metaphysical coherency of the Galápagos. Four motifs pervade the sketches: imagery of hell and penal servitude, unreality and enchantment, humanity either degraded or triumphant, and, most important, the symbol of the tortoise.

For Melville the Galápagos Islands are a world to themselves, but a world under Satan's dominion. Sketches First through Tenth are permeated by images of heat, aridity, and destruction by fire—motifs appropriate to the organically and spiritually dead landscape of hell. In the opening sketch Melville likens the isles to "five-and-twenty heaps of cinders" and to a group of extinct volcanoes, "looking much as the world at large might, after a penal conflagration" (*SW*, p. 49). The image of the burned-out cinder is carried through the sketches, and Sketch Tenth closes, fittingly, with one last variation on this motif. In his *Journal of a Cruise* (1815) Porter had recorded a doggerel epitaph placed over a sailor's lonely grave on one of the islands. Melville modified the epitaph, especially its conventionalized last line, "I hope in heaven my soul to rest," to fit the infernal character of the Galápagos landscape:

> Oh, Brother Jack, as you pass by,
> As you are now, so once was I.
> Just so game, and just so gay,
> But now, alack, they've stopped my pay.
> No more I peep out of my blinkers,
> Here I be—tucked in with clinkers!
>
> (*SW*, p. 117)

Nothing living can endure long on the Galápagos, Melville suggests. Like the Apples of Sodom "after touching," the islands themselves have the appearance of "once living things malignly crumbled from ruddiness into ashes" (*SW*, p. 53). Also, the air enveloping the archipelago threatens to destroy any living thing that seeks habitation there, for the isles are "blighted as by a continual sirocco and burning breeze." In what is probably the most striking single image in the sketches, Melville describes the unchangeable desolation of these lands: "Like split Syrian gourds left withering in the sun, they are cracked by an everlasting drought beneath a torrid sky" (*SW*, p. 50).

Images of enchantment and unreality comprise the second descriptive pattern in the sketches. Baffling winds and calms and unaccountable currents give the Enchanted Isles their name, and the anecdote of the *Essex*, as well as the stories of Oberlus and Hunilla, include allusions to the bewitching forces at work in the archipelago. An epigraph from Spenser about the "Wandring Islands" which "to and fro do ronne" introduces Sketch First and sets the stage for commentary on the unpredictable currents in the area. Then Melville gives a paradoxical twist to the Spenserian image: "However wavering their place may seem by reason of the currents, they themselves, at least to one upon the shore, appear invariably the same: fixed, cast, glued into the very body of cadaverous death" (*SW*, p. 53).

Part of the unreal quality of the isles originates, the narrator observes, from their powers to work transformations on their inhabitants. Tradition has it that all wicked sea-officers are at death metamorphosed into Galápagos tortoises, but a more dramatic transformation involves towering Rock Rodondo itself. At a distance sailors often mistake the birdlime-streaked mountain for "some Spanish Admiral's ship, stacked up with glittering canvas. *Sail ho! Sail ho! Sail ho!* from all three masts. But, coming nigh, the enchanted frigate is transformed apace into a craggy keep" (*SW*, p. 61). The narrator, too, as I have noted, would continue to feel the effects of Galápagos enchantments even when thousands of miles away.

In the third unifying imagery pattern Melville focuses upon the character and experiences of the human habitants of the archipelago. Here the opposing tensions in the sketches are especially noticeable. At the upper end of the islands' scale of humanity is Hunilla, who triumphed heroically over the degradation that she was forced to undergo; at the lower end is the Dog King of Charles Isle, and, more particularly, the hermit Oberlus, to whom degradation and depravity came naturally. Somewhere in the middle of the scale are the buccaneers, those free and roving cavalier souls who sought out the islands as a "bower of ease." Freely improvising from a passage in Colnett's *A Voyage to the South Atlantic* (1798), Melville quotes from a "sentimental voyager" who had once strolled through the crumbling remains of a buccaneer lounging-place on Albemarle Isle. "With a rusty dagger-fragment in one hand, and a bit of a wine-jar in another," he had sat down on a ruinous green sofa of stone and turf and "long and deeply" pondered the character of the buccaneers. His comments reaffirm Melville's attraction to the bachelor life-style, even as they also suggest the Ishmaelian dualistic vision of reality:

> Could it be possible that [the buccaneers] robbed and murdered one day, reveled the next, and rested themselves by turning meditative philosophers, rural poets, and seat-builders on the third? Not very improbable, after all. For consider the vacillations of a man. Still, strange as it may seem, I must also abide by the more charitable thought; namely, that among these adventurers were some gentlemanly, companionable souls, capable of genuine tranquillity and virtue. (*SW*, p. 79)

Sketch Eighth and Sketch Ninth treat in diptych fashion the contrasting figures of Hunilla and Oberlus. Although Melville does not, as he would in the diptychs, overtly compare or contrast the two sketches in terms of character, event, or implication, the two works mutually illuminate and reinforce each other. Hunilla is even further ennobled when juxtaposed with Oberlus, and Oberlus seems the more degraded when compared with Hunilla.

Charles N. Watson argues persuasively that the Hunilla story, which has no source in the Galápagos legends and histories that Melville knew, is a literary reincarnation of the Agatha letters of 1852.[7] Thus it is no surprise to find that Melville's use of landscape imagery to reflect character follows the same technique—and one adapted to similar purposes—as that in the "Agatha" outline. The first important image in the sketch, like the opening description in Agatha, pictures Hunilla on a lofty cliff meditating upon the malignity of the sea; here she is forced to witness helplessly the death of her husband and her brother when their catamaran breaks up on the shoals. Not yet comprehending what she has seen, Hunilla views the event as "some sham tragedy on the stage." The branches she looks through form an "oval frame" for the scene, the

7. "Melville's Agatha and Hunilla: A Literary Reincarnation," *English Language Notes*, 6 (Dec. 1968), 114–18.

sea looks "painted," and the men are so far away that no sound is heard (*SW*, pp. 90, 91). "Death in a silent picture; a dream of the eye," Melville terms the tragedy.

But the stark reality of the event becomes apparent to Hunilla as time passes. The captain who had originally left the woman and her loved ones to hunt tortoises on the island fails to return as promised, and Melville uses a series of images to denote concurrently the relentless passage of time and Hunilla's amazing fortitude and endurance. The ceaseless, "all-pervading monotone" of the sea, although it reminds her of the natural forces which murdered her men, also helps condition her hope that, as wave follows wave, so shall day follow day until the ship, at last, returns. A piece of hollow cane, which had drifted up on the beach, serves as a second time symbol. Notched by Hunilla as her calendar, the first groove the deepest but the last one very faint, the reed is the poetic and metaphoric counterpart of her soul, worn by agony yet unbroken: "Long ground between the sea and land, upper and nether stone, the unvarnished substance was filed bare, and wore another polish now, one with itself, the polish of its agony.... The panel of the days was deeply worn—the long tenth notches half effaced, as alphabets of the blind. Ten thousand times the longing widow had traced her finger over the bamboo—dull flute, which played on, gave no sound ..." (*SW*, pp. 94–95).

Hunilla stopped marking the cane after the one hundred and eightieth day because, the narrator implies, on that day she underwent her worst trial of humanity: she was raped by sailors from a passing ship. Nevertheless, she managed to endure long after that, until rescued by the crew of the narrator's vessel. In emphasizing the significance of her triumph over disgrace, pain, and grief, Melville says that in Hunilla's pride was her strength—"nature's pride subduing nature's torture." And when she is at length returned to her Peruvian home town, the author establishes one final symbol for her spiritual fortitude: "The last seen of lone Hunilla she was passing into Payta town, riding upon a small gray ass; and before her on the ass's shoulders, she eyed the jointed workings of the beast's armorial cross" (SW, p. 101). Like the bamboo reed, the symbol of Christ gives back to the woman yet another image of herself; although raped at Satan's hand, on the satanic Galápagos isles, she had not yielded her spirit to the powers of blackness. As Ronald Mason observes, the Christian reference which closes the story "has the effect of elevating Hunilla into a universal symbol, in whom suffering and dignity combine to ennoble humanity, which without her detached stoicism would be degraded as well as destroyed."[8]

The contrasting figure of Oberlus, in the next sketch, represents the level of degradation to which a man lacking "detached stoicism" can fall. Porter's *Journal of a Cruise* appears the most likely source for Oberlus, a red-haired Irishman whose real name was Patrick Watkins. Both Porter and Melville describe Oberlus as degenerated to the level of the tortoises, although Melville adds the ironic qualification that "the sole superiority of Oberlus over the tortoises was his possession of a larger capacity of degradation" (SW, p. 104). Some of Oberlus's satanic characteristics were mentioned by Porter, but Melville's imagery is for the most part his own. This foul creature inhabits a "den of lava and clinkers," and his "beast-like" form is covered only with rags. With an Hawthornean touch, Melville adds: "So warped and crooked was his strange nature, that the very handle of his hoe seemed gradually to have shrunk and twisted in his grasp, being a wretched bent stick, elbowed more like a savage's war-sickle than a civilized hoe-handle. . . . When planting, his whole aspect and all his gestures were so malevolently and uselessly sinister and secret, that he seemed rather in act [sic] of dropping poison into wells than potatoes into soil" (SW, pp. 103–04).

Oberlus's physical and mortal stature clearly contrasts with

8. *The Spirit Above the Dust*, p. 190.

Hunilla's, and so do his deeds. He establishes himself as the misanthropic ruler of Hood's Isle and, acting "out of mere delight in tyranny and cruelty," captures some errant seamen, forcing them into slavery. Two or three die in the "initiating process," and the survivors become "wholly corrupted to his hands" (SW, p. 108). Oberlus had planned to use his wretched army to massacre a passing ship's crew and then capture their vessel, but he and his men steal a longboat instead and thus leave the island. In contrast to Hunilla, who had entered Payta as Christ entered Jerusalem, Oberlus arrives in Payta in a singularly untriumphant manner: his "devilish aspect" makes him a "highly suspicious character," and he is soon seized and thrown into jail. Melville ends the sketch with an ironic inversion of the Christian theme which had closed the Chola widow story: "And here [in prison], for a long time, Oberlus was seen; the central figure of a mongrel and assassin band; a creature whom it is religion to detest, since it is philanthropy to hate a misanthrope" (SW, p. 112).

The final and most important motif in the sketches is the symbol of the tortoise. This reptile is the central force for resolving the major tensions in the sketches: those between degradation and triumph, between life and death, and between the real and the supernatural. With the tortoise, "The Encantadas" synthesize as art and as philosophy.

In the first place, the tortoise is a symbol of the eternal punishment which is the isles' peculiar curse. The narrator notes, "there is something strangely self-condemned in the appearance of these creatures. Lasting sorrow and penal hopelessness are in no animal form so suppliantly expressed as in theirs; while the thought of their wonderful longevity does not fail to enhance the impression" (SW, p. 53). Thus the tortoise is a suitable emblem for the evil powers of enchantment that pervade the isles, for the tortoises seem "the victims of a penal, or malignant, or perhaps a downright diabolical enchanter." So observes the narrator after discovering that a huge turtle left on deck had tried all night to force a passage through the foot of the foremast; "that strange infatuation of hopeless toil which so often possesses them" can be ascribed only to an evil wizard's conjurations (*SW*, p. 58).

At the same time, however, the tortoise represents the Hunilla-like qualities of heroic triumph and endurance. In his provocative study of primitivism and symbolism, James Baird asserts that the tortoise in "The Encantadas" becomes "the strongest of all [Melville's] autotypes of the primeval world," save for the sea and the great whale.[9] For Baird the most significant "strength" of the tortoise symbol is that of timelessness. Melville calls the creatures "antediluvian" and comments that the "great feeling inspired by these creatures was that of age:— dateless, indefinite endurance." As Baird puts it, the tortoise "touches the world of ancient reptilian life."[10] What other creature lives as long as the Encantadas tortoise, Melville asks, and "What other bodily being possesses such a citadel wherein to resist the assaults of Time?" (*SW*, p. 57). Yet it is this very quality of ageless endurance which reminds the narrator, even during "scenes of social merriment," of his own ephemeral existence. Like the figure of Hunilla, the turtle symbolizes the power of the life force, even as it makes one aware of his own proximity to death.

Finally, the tortoise is a complex synthesis of the basic dialectic in "The Encantadas": the contrast between reality and unreality. As a symbol of reality, Melville explains in "Two Sides to a Tortoise," the tortoise has its "melancholy" side and its "bright side." The tortoise may appear grim and monstrous, and so reality, too, has its evil half. But still one cannot deny the tortoise his virtues, or life its blessings. Practically speaking, the tortoise, like the whale, serves many positive purposes. The narrator reminds us of this one evening—recalling a "wild nightmare" he had about the strange creatures the previous

9. *Ishmael* (Baltimore: Johns Hopkins Press, 1956), p. 377.
10. Ibid., p. 378.

day—when he sits down to a delicious meal of tortoise steaks and tortoise stews. And, of course, the tortoise is hunted for its oil, a source of fuel and light.

Yet the Galápagos turtle is also a strangely unreal creature, in fact a supernatural being that appears prominently in the archetypal imagery of the Orient. Melville comments that these "mystic" creatures "seemed newly crawled forth from beneath the foundations of the world. Yea, they seemed the identical tortoises whereon the Hindoo plants this total sphere" (*SW*, p. 57). During his nightmare the narrator had found himself sitting cross-legged on the foremost of three huge tortoises, with "a Brahmin similarly mounted upon either side, forming a tripod of foreheads which upheld the universal cope." Baird responds to the philosophic force of this Melvillean symbol: "At the foundation of the universe, the tortoise is older even than the whale in which Vishnu came to earth to search the depths of the waters for the Sacred Vedas. He is older than every other emblem of Ishmael's art; and on his back rests all—the wildness and the wonder, the sorrow and the desolation of man's God-made existence."[11] Like the whale, the tortoise remains larger than all of the meanings man can find for it; so, too, the Encantadas.

11. Ibid., p. 381.

VIII

Form as Vision: The Ironic Quest

The Quest as Myth

The pervasiveness of the quest in myth and literature has made for considerable looseness of definition. Characters are always "in quest" of something, whether a specific object (a golden fleece) or a more abstract goal ("success"), and our concept of the quest seems to vary from tale to tale. For a minimal kind of expectation, though, most would agree with W. H. Auden that "To look for a lost collar button is not a true quest." Rather, "to go in quest means to look for something of which one has, as yet, no experience."[1] As a literary form, Auden continues, the quest is persistently appealing because the experiences of quest-heroes are recognized as somehow symbolic of our own.[2]

Joseph Campbell explains that the symbolical themes of the quest, and thus its meaning, derive to a considerable extent from the mythic patterns and formulas that constitute its morphology. Typically, a fledgling hero is called to undertake a journey into an unknown realm, in search of an object or person normally of supernatural power. Reaching the goal matures the hero or regenerates him, physically or spiritually, and he then returns to his own world with the capacity to give boons to his fellowman. Within each of the three primary stages of

1. "The Quest Hero," *Texas Quarterly*, 4 (Winter 1961), 81.
2. Ibid., p. 82.

the quest—departure, initiation, and return—Campbell identifies the individual steps along the adventurer's path. In the first stage, typically, a herald calls the hero to his task, "helpers" either natural or supernatural provide directions or assistance, and the hero must cross the "threshold of adventure" into an unknown landscape where he will encounter mysterious powers at work. As part of his initiation, stage two, the quester traditionally must undergo a series of trials and ordeals (again, helpers may aid him) before his regeneration. A spiritually transfiguring marriage with a goddess or the apotheosis of the hero are characteristic forms which the quest takes when the adventurer arrives at his goal. In the return phase the quester must successfully journey back to society and share with mankind the special knowledge or spiritual boon he has received.[3]

Melville's imagination drew instinctively upon these archetypal elements of the quest as he gave his novels and tales aesthetic form. Yet in every case, Melville, always the skeptic, found not triumph but irony in his questers' experience. I have discussed Melville's use of the quest in "Fragments from a Writing-Desk," and, of course, the ironic search is basic to the structure of *Mardi* and *Moby-Dick*. Of the magazine tales, only "The Happy Failure," "Cock-A-Doodle-Doo!" and "The Piazza" are morphologically complete quests; once again, in each of these stories Melville sees the quest in ironic terms. Melville uses one kind of irony in "The Happy Failure," where an old man does not achieve his goal but is nevertheless morally rejuvenated by his quest. But the failures depicted in "Cock-A-Doodle-Doo!" and "The Piazza" are not the result of quest-

3. See *Hero with a Thousand Faces* (Cleveland: World Publishing Co., 1956), pp. 30–251, passim. Auden offers a slightly different quest morphology in "The Quest Hero" (p. 83), identifying six essential elements: (1) a precious object and/or person to be found; (2) a long journey to find the quest-object; (3) a hero of right breeding or character; (4) a test or series of tests which only the hero can accomplish; (5) guardians of the object which the hero must overcome; (6) helpers, either animal or human, whose special powers assist the hero.

heroes falling short of their mark. Rather, these two quests are psychological and emotional measures of the ineffectuality of the narrators *as* quest-heroes.

As we have seen, the quester in "Cock-A-Doodle-Doo!" found the rooster he was searching for, but used its transcendental crowing to justify or reinforce his own inadequacies. Beating a hasty retreat before a truth he could not face, he became a prophet of delusion and false hope for others. In "The Piazza," which is at once a quest and a complex parable of creativity, the quester also finds the quest-object; yet he refuses to admit to himself that the quest does not bring about the personal transformation he so desperately needs. Furthermore, like the quester in "Cock-A-Doodle-Doo!" he violates the spirit of the quest by not communicating his experiences honestly to mankind, in order to educate others about the perils of the quest and reveal the psychological and spiritual demands made on the quester.

"The Happy Failure": The Paradox of Defeat

Despite its facile artistry, "The Happy Failure" (*Harper's*, July 1854) illustrates the relationship between the mythical patterns of the quest and its meaning. The tale is narrated by the flinty old inventor's young nephew, whose character Melville does not choose to develop; instead he retains him as an observer and as the moral center for the story. The tale is an allegory of sorts: the old uncle has for ten long years forced his Negro servant to help him build a machine which he hopes will make him a millionaire—a device to drain swamps and convert them to fertile farmland. His nephew and the servant Yorpy row the contraption ten miles upstream (one mile for each year's labor?) to "Quash Island," where he can try it without being observed. The uncle's hopes are indeed quashed when the apparatus fails to perform, and he literally almost dies from his disappointment before coming to his senses and treating his faithful servant kindly once again. The old fellow realizes that his failure has made a better person of him, and the story closes with his fervent expression of newly acquired insight: "Praise be to God for the failure!" (*SW*, p. 232). The story is structured upon the archetypal stages of the quest: a secretive and difficult journey against the current to the spot where the object of the ten-year quest will be confronted (a distant island is a traditional setting for the quester's goal); the use of "helpers" on the quest; the experience with the device itself; and, finally, the return, after the quester has undergone spiritual enlightenment. Somewhat in the manner of "The Tartarus of Maids" and "The Bell-Tower," Melville's is a symbolical tale about the machine's dominion over man; appropriately, the swamp-draining device looks satanic, like "a huge nest of anacondas and adders" (*SW*, p. 228). Critics have treated "The Happy Failure," "The Fiddler," and "Jimmy Rose" as three successive "studies in the values of failure,"[4] and Melville's famous statement in his review of the *Mosses* seems especially applicable to the meaning of the story: "But it is better to fail in originality, than to succeed in imitation. He who has never failed somewhere, that man cannot be great. Failure is the true test of greatness."[5] The uncle's quest for riches involved the designing of an "original" piece of equipment, but his failure made him a finer man. His nephew and black Yorpy rejoice in the old man's illumination, and the quest is over.

The Ironic Hero of "The Piazza"

"The Piazza," writes Richard Fogle, is a picture-story set in a "fantastically decorative frame"; the tale is in effect a study

4. The phrase is Fogle's in *Melville's Shorter Tales*, p. 58. See also Hoyle, "Melville as a Magazinist," pp. 137–44, and Joseph A. Ward, Jr., "Melville and Failure," *Emerson Society Quarterly*, 33 (IV Quarter 1963), 43–46.
5. "Hawthorne and His Mosses [Part II]," p. 146.

of stage illusion, and "the question of reality is left open."[6] Fogle's interpretation is suggestive, and it has been echoed by others. What has not been recognized, however, are the ways in which the morphology of the mythical quest controls and determines both the structure and the vision of "The Piazza." For the larger image patterns of "The Piazza" are thoroughly developed and exactly duplicate the three stages of the quest: the departure from the known, the ordeals of the hero preparatory to his initiation, and the return.

Melville's use of the ironic quest in "The Piazza" takes on even more significance when one realizes the place this story occupies in his magazine fiction as a whole. "The Piazza" was written in January or February 1856, as a prefatory sketch for the forthcoming collection of Melville's *Putnam's* stories through 1855: "Bartleby," "The Encantadas," "The Lightning-Rod Man," "The Bell-Tower," and "Benito Cereno."[7] Melville did not intend "The Piazza" to recapitulate or formally survey the five earlier tales included in the volume. It is more likely that he saw his introductory sketch as Hawthorne had viewed "The Old Manse," preface to the *Mosses*: as a portrait of the author looking out over the landscape of his own art and pondering, whimsically and seriously, the complex relationships between art and knowledge.[8]

"The Piazza," Helmbrecht Breinig has suggested, is a tale of the "fairyland" or "neutral territory" of the artist's imagination, and as such it is a commentary on the limits of art.[9] For

6. *Melville's Shorter Tales*, p. 85.
7. For an historical account of the publication of Melville's collected stories see Sealts, "The Publication of Melville's *The Piazza Tales*."
8. Donaldson, in "The Dark Truth of *The Piazza Tales*," views the tales as a related group, commenting on their general themes of perception, isolation, and human servitude.
9. In "The Destruction of Fairyland: Melville's 'Piazza' in the Tradition of the American Imagination," *ELH*, 35 (June 1968), 254–83, Breinig discusses the tension between the actual world and the artist's "fairyland" in Irving, Hawthorne, and Melville. My comments on "The Piazza" to some extent parallel Breinig's. Several scholars have discussed the similarities between Hawthorne's "The Old Manse"

absolute freedom of imagination is always denied the artist, and hence art must remain at best a compromise with reality. "The Piazza" also implies that the artist is denied final insight into the truth he would portray; in this respect the story as ironic quest parallels and subtly comments on the *Piazza Tales* and on Melville's short fiction as a whole. Even as Melville's narrators cannot define the "real" Bartleby, the truth about Cereno, or the ultimate meaning of the enchanted Galápagos, so must Melville acknowledge the limits of his own epistemology. As a study of the artist's ironic quest for the fairyland of art and for the realms of truth, "The Piazza" seems to represent Melville's whole career as a fiction-maker.

The essential pattern of the tale is the search for the woman, an archetypal quest motif. Melville's narrator is an artist with a literary turn of mind, and his quest appropriately takes the form of a symbolical search for Spenser's Una, princess of truth; ironically, however, he finds only Tennyson's melancholy Mariana, slowly passing her life away in isolated retreat.

Sitting on his newly built piazza, Melville's narrator one day observes a spot of radiance "mysteriously snugged away" on an upper slope of Mount Greylock. Imagining it to be "some haunted ring where fairies dance" or a fairy cottage, he decides that it heralds for him an unimaginable reward, at the very least an encounter with a fairy princess, could he but journey there. Yet almost a year passes while sickness keeps the hero from his quest.

The circumstances which bring him, finally, to leave the security of his home in search of the fairy maiden are an inversion of the heroic challenge or call to adventure which the traditional quester must accept; furthermore, the imagery of departure ironically reflects his lack of potential for success. Judith Slater argues that Melville's quester journeys to the

---

and "The Piazza" as prefatory sketches. See especially my essay "The Minor Fiction of Hawthorne and Melville" (cited above), Christy's dissertation, "The Shock of Recognition: A Psycho-Literary Study of Hawthorne's Influence on Melville's Short Fiction," and Breinig.

mountain largely because he seeks an escape from a mild emotional upset, caused in part by his slow convalescence but precipitated by a disconcerting discovery in his garden.[10] As in "Cock-A-Doodle-Doo!" a fitful preoccupation with disease and nature's ugliness introduces the quest, foreshadowing neither feats of arms nor valiant action for the quest-hero:

> . . . I could not bear to look upon a Chinese creeper of my adoption . . . which . . . had burst out in starry bloom, but now, if you removed the leaves a little, showed millions of strange, cankerous worms, which, feeding upon those blossoms, so shared their blessed hue, as to make it un-blessed evermore—worms, whose germs had doubtless lurked in the very bulb which, so hopefully, I had planted: in this ingrate peevishness of my weary convalescence, was I sitting there; when, suddenly looking off, I saw the golden mountain-window. . . . Fairies there, thought I . . . the queen of fairies . . . at any rate, some glad mountain-girl . . . it will cure this weariness, to look on her. . . . (SW, pp. 443–44)

The narrator's "peevishness" has distorted the spirit of the quest. Even though he seems to accept Spenser's injunction that fairyland must be voyaged to "with faith" (SW, p. 444), he does not view his quest as a courageous endeavor to bring light and truth to himself and to others. In fact, the death-in-life imagery of the flower and the fact that his journey is essentially "westward" (SW, p. 444) anticipate the death of his dreams of fairyland.

In crossing the threshold that separates the known world from the unknown, the hero must overcome obstacles and survive the "perilous passage" before he can experience the mystical union with the woman. Melville's protagonist fights no trolls or dragons, however; his major challenge is afforded by the lengthiness and difficulty of his horseback climb up the mountain. At one point Melville effectively suits form to theme

10. "The Domestic Adventurer in Melville's Tales," p. 278.

by means of an exhausting 230-word sentence describing the ascent, punctuated by the word "on" as an adverbial conjunction (*SW*, p. 445). The journey is mildly perilous, too, and the narrator runs the risk of "enchantment" along the way: his path grows darker and more obscure, he encounters cattle seemingly under a spell, and he finds a deserted saw mill and other signs that man had long since forsaken the region he traverses.

Archetypally, the protagonist is given assistance by helpers. Roadside golden rods, "as guide-posts," aid him in effecting his passage, and he is joined by an old ram with a crumpled horn and then by flights of yellow birds to pilot him at least part way through the dark but "luring" woods. Yet soon the birds disappear and so does Aries the ram, who, "renouncing me now for some lost soul, wheeled, and went his wiser way." "Forbidding and forbidden ground—to him," the narrator adds (*SW*, p. 445). Eventually the protagonist must leave his horse behind and make his way on foot.

At last, among "fantastic rocks" the hero discovers a little cottage and a maiden within. From the piazza of his valley home the quester has reached the setting for his supposedly transfiguring vision, but it is no coincidence that Marianna's cabin is reminiscent of the poor Marylander's hut in "Cock-A-Doodle-Doo!" Both are shabby and dilapidated, and they are suitably depressing dwellings for the ironic epiphanies that the questers in the stories experience. Hoping to find his princess of truth inside the cottage, the narrator confronts instead a lonely and disillusioned maiden who laments the weariness of her life. In his 1830 poem Tennyson describes Mariana as grown "aweary" in waiting for a lover who would never come; the poet also depicts her loathing for the bright sunbeams that penetrate her chambers and mentions a solitary tree which casts a shadow on her bed and brow. Melville uses Tennyson's motifs to reinforce his imagery of isolation and unfulfilled longing: his Marianna also laments her "weariness," and young men never visit her cottage. Furthermore, Melville's maiden tries to shut out the sun which blinds her, and a nearby tree, whose friendly shadow used to soothe her weariness, had been struck down by lightning. Both writers also picture mossy, time-worn, and weather-beaten cottages—symbols of the psychologically fatigued maidens who inhabit them.

Whereas the Grail quester has a vision of holiness and spiritual joy in the Grail house at the end of his journey, the narrator of "The Piazza" finds only sadness and melancholy. Yet the real irony of the story, as in "Cock-A-Doodle-Doo!" lies in the narrator's choosing to ignore the implications of his quest and refusing to share the truth of his experiences with mankind. The movement of the quest is traditionally from darkness to light, but Melville's narrator evades what has been revealed to him on his journey—that the world does not necessarily gratify one's needs, and that the artist's fantasies cannot be made real. The protagonist had sought "Truth" as well as the restoration of his aesthetic sensibilities, which had been jarred by finding the worms in his Chinese creeper. But he had discovered only Marianna's melancholy and her ironic longing: she had yearned to visit the narrator's own house in the valley, imagining it to be a marble mansion occupied by a "happy being."

The quester lets Marianna keep her illusions, but his mistake lies in trying to keep his own as well. That he would rather deny his discoveries than confront them and share them with others is indicated when he abruptly breaks off his dialogue with Marianna, shortly after she reveals her ironic wish:

—Enough. Launching my yawl no more for fairy-land, I stick to the piazza. It is my box-royal; and this amphi-theatre [of the surrounding mountains], my theatre of San Carlo. Yes, the scenery is magical—the illusion so complete. And Madam Meadow Lark, my prima donna, plays her grand engagement here; and, drinking in her sunrise note, which, Memnon-like, seems struck from the golden window, how far from me the weary face behind it.

But, every night, when the curtain falls, truth comes in with darkness. No light shows from the mountain. To and fro I walk the piazza deck, haunted by Marianna's face, and many as real a story. (*SW*, p. 453)

Amid the narrator's comments on his "box-royal" one finds certain disquieting notes. First of all, he hints that his quest may not really have happened after all; there are other stories he could tell as "real" as this one. Was the Marianna episode just a "story," then? But even if the quest were imaginary, or were only an artist's dream of fairyland, the quester could still have found truth or inspiration in it; dream quests abound in folklore. Not so with Melville's hero, for even as he had avoided telling Marianna the truth so he keeps himself from squarely facing reality. As Professor Slater puts it, there is something "unsatisfactory" about the narrator's realizing by night the truth that "comes in with darkness" and claiming to enjoy the "illusion" by day. Thus Melville's artist lives in a "divided realm" and "suffers from his inability to reconcile the halves."[11]

As an ironic quest, "The Piazza" is finally more than a parable about the artist's failure to achieve Truth or the fairyland of the imagination. If, as Auden claims, the quest holds universal meanings, then the weakness of Melville's quest-hero symbolizes every man's limitations and self-doubts, however disguised. Thus Melville's rhetoric of fiction in his tale compels us to read, almost against our wills, about ourselves.

11. Ibid., p. 279.

EPILOGUE

The Short Fiction in Perspective

In experimenting with short fiction in the middle 1850's, Melville found new artistic strength. Obliged by the form of the magazine tale to compress and focus his creative powers, he saw more clearly than he had before the effect of discipline on craftsmanship. As a result, there is very little wasted motion in the magazine stories, and some of the tales reveal a verbal facility unrivalled anywhere in his works. The onesided conversations in "Bartleby," the comic interaction of characters in "I and My Chimney" and "The Apple-Tree Table," or the imagistic art of "The Encantadas" and "The Piazza" constitute some of Melville's very best writing; in terms of originality and inventiveness, the short fiction is as rich as *Mardi* or *Moby-Dick*. Furthermore, Melville enjoyed himself as a magazinist. There was no falling off of energy, and many of the tales convey the same sense of exuberance and delight in literary creation that we find in Taji's and Ishmael's greatest improvisational moments.

Yet it is the relationship between vision and technique in the short stories that makes them among Melville's most significant literary achievements. Invariably, in the short tales, Melville puts human personality and reflexes at the center of art. It is a character's comic, pathetic, melodramatic, or even neurotic response to experience, or his failure to respond at all to the things around him, that forms the immediate world of Melville's tales. The other world of his short fiction is the reader's. The distance between these two worlds varies in each story, but there is always a noticeable degree of separation, and hence irony. For in writing short stories for the magazines Melville discovered the leverage available in the consistent use of rhetorical irony. In his juvenilia and the novels he had seen some of the ironic possibilities of first-person narration, but he had to watch his metaphysical crescendos in *Moby-Dick* and *Pierre* fall on deaf ears before he was ready to learn the lessons that irony could teach.

The ironic mode was essentially a subversive one, Melville realized. Employing a narrator as a potentially false guide for the reader was artistically perilous, but in the short tales Melville mastered the technique, often using it more subtly than had Poe or Irving, in fact. Behind the persona of a methodical Wall Street lawyer, or an indolent old hearty before his fireplace, or a well-intentioned sea captain, Melville tested the platitudes and assumptions of his reading public; yet always, as he had in the great novels, he revealed a higher order of truth or reality in place of man's conventionalisms.

If the reader of Melville's short fiction pays too much attention to the sentimental, humorous, or melodramatic surface of the stories his narrators tell, he will fail to see the author's more complex philosophical and aesthetic intentions. Melville's short fiction narrators were not, as Ishmael so often tended to be, just authorial mouthpieces; thus the Romantic vision of the short stories differs from that of *Moby-Dick*. The truth may be finally inscrutable, Ishmael had pretended in 1851, but let us see how near we can come to it anyhow; as a Romantic Melville admired any man who "dived" deeply. However, in "Bartleby," "Cock-A-Doodle-Doo!" or "Benito Cereno," the protagonist often fails to understand that there is a truth to be dived for, or, if he thinks he has glimpses of it, fails to see that what he is actually diving for is the truth about himself.

Melville's experiments with the rhetorical methods of the magazine tale also have implications for the two novels that he published in the last half of the 1850's. The metaphysician had turned more completely to irony and satire after *Moby-*

Dick, and economic, social, and political criticism contribute to the texture and technique of the magazine stories as well as to *Israel Potter* (1855) and *The Confidence-Man* (1857). *Israel Potter* was written as a magazine serial for *Putnam's*; predictably, it is an episodical adventure tale, characteristically Melvillean in its focus on an isolato subject to the vagaries of fate. In some ways, too, this book is a warm-up exercise for *The Confidence-Man*. Melville's satirical sketch of the archetypal American Ben Franklin, and his definitely mixed portraits of Ethan Allen and John Paul Jones, prepare the ground for the more universalized criticism of the "western spirit" of entrepreneurish America, and the sardonic undercutting of human nature in general, in the next novel.

The Confidence-Man is a difficult book to evaluate. Most readers acknowledge its ingeniousness and its amazingly rich mythic and allegorical texture. Yet Melville's proliferation of ambiguities and contradictions has made impatient even the most circumspect of critics, including those, like Daniel G. Hoffman, who are most dazzled by the novel's precociousness.[1] The problem with *The Confidence-Man* may be that Melville had carried his short fiction experiments with indirection and rhetorical irony too far. Like "The Piazza," *The Confidence-Man* raises important questions about the limits of art; but, in his novel, Melville may unintentionally have kept too carefully hidden the truths or insights that he wished to convey.

Leon Howard has suggested that the novel, composed in 1856, was probably intended as another serial in *Putnam's*.[2] Internal evidence indicates, in fact, that Melville wrote the first half of the manuscript as a series of separate installments for *Putnam's*, perhaps one installment for each of the first seven incarnations of the confidence-man. With the introduction of the cosmopolitan, Melville's scope and direction seem

1. See Chapter 14, "The Confidence-Man: His Masquerade," in *Form and Fable in American Fiction* (New York: Oxford Univ. Press, 1961).
2. *Herman Melville*, pp. 227–28.

to have changed; the work grew into a book-length satiric allegory on confidence, belief, and human nature. Initially inspired by Melville's reading or hearing about a celebrated New York con-artist,[3] the novel is structured around multiple encounters with what appear to be multiple strangers. In terms of form, *The Confidence-Man* is "Bartleby" amplified: the mysterious scrivener is replaced by a series of mysterious strangers, and the lawyer by the numerous passengers who try, unsuccessfully, to interpret the strangers' significance.

As Melville developed the ironic possibilities of his novel, he tried one more rhetorical experiment.[4] If, as the book suggests, this is a world in which philanthropists and misanthropes, the real and the artificial, and God and the Devil are indistinguishable, then to be consistent with his vision the novelist should take special care to conceal truth behind falsity. As scholars have frequently pointed out, Melville's revisions, narrative digressions, and interpolated stories-within-stories seem to deny the possibility that anything can be stated as incontrovertible fact, as unvarying truth.

A notable instance of Melville's conscious distancing of the reader from reality is "The Story of the Unfortunate Man," a narrative several removes from "the truth." Melville's semi-omniscient narrator tells in his own words a tale about John Ringman and his wife Goneril that he had heard from the merchant, who had in turn learned details of the story from the confidence-man in the gray coat, as well as from the confidence-man Ringman himself. Of course, whatever narrative

3. For a thorough analysis of Melville's central source for the confidence-man, see Johannes D. Bergmann, "The Original Confidence Man," *American Quarterly*, 21 (Fall 1969), 560–77.
4. My general argument here parallels that of several critics who have analyzed the rhetorical patterns of the novel. See especially John G. Cawelti, "Some Notes on the Structure of *The Confidence-Man*," *American Literature*, 29 (Nov. 1957), 278–88; Edgar A. Dryden, *Melville's Thematics of Form* (Baltimore: Johns Hopkins Univ. Press, 1968), pp. 151ff.; Merlin Bowen, "Tactics of Indirection in Melville's *The Confidence-Man*," *Studies in the Novel*, 1 (Winter 1969), 401–20.

Ringman related was probably a total fabrication to begin with, designed to elicit sympathy. The problem here is that Melville's rhetorical technique raises too many ambiguities simultaneously. Is it Melville's point that inhuman creatures like Goneril could be real, and that an originally innocent John Ringman could be transformed into a satanic con-man by such a female? The joke may be on the reader, finally, in that he is asked to puzzle over a contradictory, and perhaps intentionally meaningless, episode.

As the veil of darkness draws down on the last chapter of *The Confidence-Man*, the novel symbolically becomes its own shroud; the reader, quite literally, is left standing in the dark about the meaning Melville intended for his novel. In the magazine stories, however, Melville provides the reader with at least a glimmer of the truth that he seeks to portray—even if this truth is that man is not privileged to know the final shape of reality.

Melville wrote no tales or novels for three decades after the publication of *The Confidence-Man*; poetry and reminiscence occupied the leisure of his later years. When he did turn his hand again to prose fiction and worked up *Billy Budd* out of the retrospective prose-poetry sketching that was going into *John Marr and Other Sailors* (1888), his rhetoric was different from that of the short stories or *The Confidence-Man*. For his experiments with rhetorical irony, as a dominant fictional mode, were over.[5] In *Billy Budd* Melville readopted the editorial-omniscient vision of *Moby-Dick* and brought into complex synthesis portraits of three phenomenal men, each of whom must act out his part on a stage that fate and man's laws have spread before him. The clustering of chapters around

---

5. Fogle was the first critic to argue persuasively against the ironic view of *Billy Budd*; see "*Billy Budd*—Acceptance or Irony," *Tulane Studies in English*, 8 (1958), 107–13. More recently, Edward Rosenberry broadened the implications of Fogle's contention that the novel is Aristotelian rather than rhetorical irony; see "The Problem of *Billy Budd*," *PMLA*, 80 (Dec. 1965), 489–98.

each of the three characters, whose actions are viewed against the backdrop of life on a man-of-war, parallels on a smaller scale the form of *Moby-Dick*—where the nature and behavior of Ahab, the crew, and the white whale are analyzed by Ishmael in the context of whaling as an industry and as a way of existence. As drama and exposition alternate in *Billy Budd*, the narrator becomes again a kind of omniscient stage manager and a voice for the author, exploring the implications of character and event.

Examining Billy, Vere, and Claggart in turn, the narrator acknowledges "mysteries of iniquity" when he finds them but also draws conclusions where he can. Like Ishmael, he openly and thoughtfully explores with the reader the tragic irony of the story: that man's limited perceptions or his psychological makeup condition his actions, and that in this complex world these actions can often have fatal results. After the ironic confessional mode of his short stories, and the contradictory posing of *The Confidence-Man*, Melville had returned to the methods and themes of earlier days. His literary growth as a fiction writer had come full circle, and was complete.

Index

Themes and characters in Melville's short fiction are not indexed; the emphasis is placed on his technique, motifs, sources, and analogues. Except where noted, the terms indexed below refer to Melville's works.